Mastering
American Indian Law

Mastering
American Indian Law

Angelique Townsend EagleWoman

ASSOCIATE PROFESSOR OF LAW AND
JAMES E. ROGERS FELLOW IN AMERICAN INDIAN LAW,
UNIVERSITY OF IDAHO COLLEGE OF LAW

Stacy L. Leeds

DEAN AND PROFESSOR OF LAW,
UNIVERSITY OF ARKANSAS SCHOOL OF LAW

CAROLINA ACADEMIC PRESS
Durham, North Carolina

Copyright © 2013
Carolina Academic Press
All Rights Reserved.

Library of Congress Cataloging in Publication Data

EagleWoman, Angelique Townsend.
 Mastering American Indian law / Angelique Townsend EagleWoman and
Stacy L. Leeds.
   pages cm. -- (Carolina Academic Press mastering series)
 Includes bibliographical references and index.
 ISBN 978-1-59460-329-7 (alk. paper)
 1. Indians of North America--Legal status, laws, etc. I. Leeds, Stacy L.,
1971- II. Title.

 KF8205.E225 2013
 340.5'27308997--dc23

                          2013018046

                    Carolina Academic Press
                        700 Kent Street
                      Durham, NC 27701
                  Telephone (919) 489-7486
                     Fax (919) 493-5668
                      www.cap-press.com

            Printed in the United States of America

*For the current and future generations of Indigenous peoples
and all peoples to envision a better common future.
With appreciation to my tiospa, my Oyate, and all those who
have inspired me to continue on this journey in the law.
— Angelique Townsend EagleWoman
(Wambdi A. WasteWin)*

*To continued community empowerment and
a bright future for our sons Maverick and Hunter.
— Stacy L. Leeds*

Contents

Series Editor's Foreword

The Carolina Academic Press Mastering Series is designed to provide you with a tool that will enable you to easily and efficiently "master" the substance and content of law school courses. Throughout the series, the focus is on quality writing that makes legal concepts understandable. As a result, the series is designed to be easy to read and is not unduly cluttered with footnotes or cites to secondary sources.

In order to facilitate student mastery of topics, the Mastering Series includes a number of pedagogical features designed to improve learning and retention. At the beginning of each chapter, you will find a "Roadmap" that tells you about the chapter and provides you with a sense of the material that you will cover. A "Checkpoint" at the end of each chapter encourages you to stop and review the key concepts, reiterating what you have learned. Throughout the book, key terms are explained and emphasized. Finally, a "Master Checklist" at the end of each book reinforces what you have learned and helps you identify any areas that need review or further study.

We hope that you will enjoy studying with, and learning from, the Mastering Series.

Russell L. Weaver
Professor of Law & Distinguished University Scholar
University of Louisville, Louis D. Brandeis School of Law

Mastering
American Indian Law

Chapter 1

Introduction to American Indian Law

Roadmap

- Understand that American Indian Law refers to two bodies of law: law created by Tribal Nations and law created by the U.S. government.
- Know the legal basis for tribal membership and federal recognition as an American Indian.
- Learn that tribal governance and laws existed pre-contact with Europeans.
- Learn the sources of contemporary tribal law.
- Learn about the body of federal Indian law and the influences of U.S. Indian policy eras on the legal relationships between tribal governments and the U.S.

The study of American Indian law is one of the broadest fields of law due to the many and varied sources of the law that shape the field. Several large bodies of law are encompassed under the general heading "Indian law." First, Tribal Nations pass their own laws and have developed extensive materials that compose Indian law. Second, the United States has developed a field of federal Indian law with an entire section of the U.S. Code dedicated to the federal statutes enacted in the subject area. Third, other legal sources for Indian law include state laws, agreements, regulations passed by U.S. federal and state regulatory bodies, judicial decisions, and administrative rulings. Fourth, the international character of the interaction between Tribes and the United States and the European powers precedent to the U.S. have on-going relevance to Indian law through the application of international indigenous legal principles.

In *Mastering American Indian Law,* you will be introduced to the primary principles formed from tribal governance and tribal interaction with the United States, labeled "Indian law." With over 560 federally-recognized Tribes, the laws of Tribes will be discussed in summary form and specifics given to highlight certain important characteristics where appropriate. This introductory chapter will introduce you to the U.S. Indian policy eras that provide a structure for comprehending the oscillating policies of federal laws in this field. Use this book as a broad comprehensive resource with the understanding that the law is constantly changing as new laws are adopted, cases are ruled upon by courts, and new agreements are reached refining the relationships between Tribes and other governments. In the final chapter, we will provide a discussion on the emerging importance of international indigenous human rights norms that may lead to new developments for tribal governments and individuals.

Introductory Note: Determining Who Is an "Indian" under the Law

As a general note, the English term "American Indian," or simply "Indian," has become common due to its use as a term in federal laws for the aboriginal peoples of mid-North America. In many areas of federal Indian law, the courts have distinguished between Indians and non-Indians. There are also distinctions noted between tribal members and non-tribal members in judicial decisions. One of the characteristics of federal Indian law is that often federal court decisions and federal laws have general applicability to all Tribal Nations on the legal issues presented, therefore one court decision can change the law on the subject area (e.g., taxation of goods sold to non-Indians) for all Tribes. The term "Native American" is customarily used in academic literature. Specific tribal names are the preference when referring to individuals or issues related to one Tribe. Additionally, the indigenous peoples of Alaska are referred to in federal law as "Alaska Natives," and the indigenous peoples of Hawaii are referred to as "Native Hawaiians." Throughout this book, reference will be made to the term employed from the source being discussed.

All federally-recognized Tribes have tribal enrollment procedures and criteria for tribal citizenship. Tribal citizenship, sometimes referred to as tribal membership, indicates tribal recognition for the individual by the Tribal Nation. Early interaction between Tribal Nations and U.S. federal officials included the development of tribal rolls by federal officials to establish who would be federally-recognized in a given Tribe, usually for treaty-guaranteed food rations or a land allotment under a federal statute. The sovereign right for Tribal Nations to determine tribal membership requirements was recognized in the U.S. Supreme Court opinion *Santa Clara Pueblo v. Martinez,* 436 U.S. 49 (1978). Today, Tribal Nations rely on the early federal rolls to determine ancestry of applicants and at times to calculate blood quantum based upon such ancestry. The U.S. government has heavily influenced tribal identification through U.S. requirements.

The largest Tribal Nation in the United States, the Cherokee Nation, does not require a minimum blood quantum amount, but does require establishing that an individual is a direct descendant of an Indian ancestor listed on one of the official federal rolls. Other Tribes may adopt guidelines of one-fourth blood quantum or may calculate all of a person's Indian ancestry from various Tribes for tribal enrollment. Every Tribal Nation has established specific citizenship criterion under tribal law. Many Tribes have also followed federal guidelines in allowing an individual to be enrolled in only one Tribe, while some are silent as to dual citizenship in other sovereigns. Without tribal enrollment, a person is not recognized as an "Indian" in the legal sense or for tribal and federal rights or benefits.

U.S. federal Indian law provides recognition of a person as an "Indian" if the person is tribally-enrolled or otherwise meets the federal blood quantum standard of one-fourth degree or more of Indian blood as calculated through the federal rolls. These criteria apply for federal services such as higher education grants under the U.S. Department of Interior's Bureau of Indian Education. In addition, the Bureau of Indian Affairs, upon request by an American Indian or Alaska Native, may issue a certificate of degree of Indian blood ("CDIB") as federal documentation. American Indians and Alaska Natives are the only people in the United States who are required to meet a blood quantum standard for proof of identity.

A. Tribal Law

For Tribal Nations, laws have been in place since time immemorial to govern internal tribal relations, external relations, commercial activities and all spheres of interaction between tribal citizens and the world at large. Many of these legal systems include moral obligations and a sense of community balance through restorative justice principles. Tribal laws, for the most part, were transmitted through oral narratives and the use of symbols to demonstrate complex societal relationships and guidelines. Segments of tribal society served as the law enforcers in tribal communities via clan systems. Leadership required dedication to the tribal laws and many Tribes also embraced a spiritual set of laws known as "natural law." In tribal communities, Indian law is the law created through tribal statutes, regulations, judicial decisions, agency determinations, and traditional customs by the Tribes themselves.

In contemporary times, Tribes generally have prioritized written laws, constitutional governmental forms, and judicial systems modeled after the United States. The transition to a hybrid U.S. governmental model largely resulted from U.S. Indian policy in the late 1930s intended to reorganize tribal governments. Size, location, and resources of Tribes have informed the type of governmental structure implemented, along with the methods of law creation, implementation, enforcement, and judicial determinations about tribal law. For example, smaller Tribes may have fewer formal processes and forums in place. A centralized forum to handle a multiplicity of legal issues would be all that is required in that instance. Larger Tribes may have extensive judicial and administrative adjudicative forums providing specialized attention to categories of legal issues. Tribal governments run the spectrum from traditional clan-based systems dating back centuries to adapted constitutional-based governments similar to the three-branch U.S. structure with executive, legislative and judicial branches.

In whatever fashion tribal governments are structured, all have written laws and dispute resolution mechanisms. The tribal side of "Indian law" takes the form comparable to other common law jurisdictions where written laws are interpreted by those performing judicial decision-making functions. Every society has a general sense of moral obligations, social behavior, and commercial interactions that influence and reside in the laws of the citizenry. Tribal governments have the ability to draw upon millennium-old ways of life handed down through oral traditions and symbol knowledge to enhance written tribal laws. Codification of tribal laws often developed through careful consideration of neighboring Tribes' general laws. In certain regions of the country, tribal written laws may bear heavy resemblances amongst neighboring Tribes. As a general rule, each Tribe has its own specific laws and judicial opinions which require research for competent representation involving a tribal legal matter.

Tribal codified laws also reflect an interaction with federal Indian law. As new federal policies are implemented nationally, particular provisions may relate to Tribes. In response, tribal leadership often codifies new laws to meet the new national policy. Thus, tribal law is fluid and part of the ongoing relationship with the United States of America. Tribal law is also responsive to tribal societal initiatives and concerns. For example, in recent years, many tribal legislatures have passed legislation implementing domestic violence and elder abuse codes to address such issues arising in tribal communities. Also, as commercial activity becomes more complex in tribal communities, tribal legislatures have enacted laws to structure business entities and handle commercial disputes.

Similarly, tribal judicial opinions originate within an existing body of law and are influenced by the decisions in other jurisdictions. In common law practice, prior court opinions have substantial bearing on the resolution of

Tribal Flags Wichita Indian Center. Photo credit Michelle C. White.

present disputes. In most tribal court systems, the order of precedential value given to prior decisions generally follows this hierarchy: 1) prior decisions of the same tribal court and the related tribal appellate courts, 2) decisions from other tribal court systems, 3) decisions from the U.S. federal court systems, and 4) decisions from U.S. state courts. This order may vary depending upon the substantive matter before the court, particularly in legal matters where tribal and state laws are very similar. For example, some Tribes have adopted the same provisions of the Uniform Commercial Code (UCC) as the surrounding state and refer to state law decisions for tribal court dispute resolution involving UCC issues.

Tribal administrative law is derived from the processes for resolution under specific tribal agencies. There are a wide-ranging number of administrative agencies that may exist within any one tribal government. A non-exclusive list of administrative agency dispute resolution processes at the tribal level may include: personnel action review boards, gaming commission hearings, tax commission review hearings, zoning commission review boards, election commission hearings, and others. Specific tribal agency regulations and tribal laws dictate whether administrative agency decisions are reviewable in the tribal judicial system.

In general, tribal law stems from three primary sources: 1) tribal statutes, 2) tribal judicial opinions, and 3) tribal agency determinations. A fourth category of tribal custom and tradition may exist in legal matters pertaining to families and domestic concerns. This fourth category may require practitioners to become familiar with expert witnesses knowledgeable in the forum's region on such matters. The primary sources of tribal law inform the majority of tribal litigation in judicial and administrative forums. Due to the close relationship between U.S. Indian policy and tribal governments, the majority of Tribes are heavily influenced by the U.S. example of statutory, administrative and judicial lawmaking.

B. U.S. Federal Indian Law

As European nations established trade relations in North America, the British established permanent settlements as colonies along the Eastern seaboard. The colonies declared their independence from Britain and formed the United States of America in 1776. The field of federal Indian law traces its roots to the trading relations Tribes developed with Great Britain and then to the successor nation, the United States. With the formation of the U.S. as a constitution-based government, the U.S. Congress was designated as the authority to manage Indian affairs for the new republic. In article 1, section eight, clause three of the U.S. Constitution, the U.S. Congress was granted the authority "To regulate Commerce with foreign Nations, and among the several States, and with the Indian Tribes." In the field of Indian law, this section of the Constitution is commonly referred to as the "Indian Commerce Clause." The U.S. Constitution adopted in 1787 also included a brief reference to "Indians not taxed" in the state apportionment clause. Throughout the history of the United States, distinct policy eras in Indian affairs have provided context for federal statutes and judicial decision-making.

1. U.S. Indian Policy Eras

United States Indian policy has been described as resembling a "wave machine" and a "pendulum," as the policy goals appear to swing between two opposite policy stances. In the early phase of the United States federal government, the foreign policy of Great Britain towards Tribal Nations was followed through treaty-making with neighboring Tribes to gain alliances and territorial rights. From this foundation of interaction with Tribal Nations, seven major policy eras have formed federal Indian law since the establishment of the United States.

These U.S. policy eras can be summarized historically as: 1) sovereign-to-sovereign relationships (1778 to mid-1800s); 2) removal era (1800s); 3) reservation era (overlaps partially with removal era, 1800s); 4) allotment/assimilation era (late 1800s to early 1900s); 5) Indian self-government (1930s to 1940s); 6) termination era (1940s to 1960s); and 7) Indian self-determination (late-1960s to present). Using the U.S. Indian policy eras as the context for understanding the, at times contradictory, laws and court opinions in federal Indian law provides a key to studying this field of law. The pendulum swing from supporting tribal government is evident in the following policy eras: sovereign-to-sovereign relationships; reservation era; Indian self-government era; and Indian self-determination/present policy. The federal laws and court cases during these policy eras tend to support tribal government formation and effectiveness, but there remain exceptions in every policy era to the general political trend. The opposing pendulum swing to the detriment of tribal government is apparent in the remaining policy eras: removal era; allotment/assimilation era; and termination era. These policy eras are shaped by some of the most detrimental federal laws and court decisions continuing to impact tribal peoples in the U.S. It is upon this changing landscape that the permutations of federal Indian law have developed over time.

a. Sovereign-to-Sovereign Relationships (1778 to mid-1800s)

As mentioned previously, the United States official policy traced its roots to Great Britain and the international practice of treaty-making between Europeans and Tribal Nations in North America. The first treaty concluded by the United States was with the Delaware Nation in 1778 and the total number of treaties entered into with Tribal Nations exceeds the four hundred mark. One of the most comprehensive online digital collections of Tribal Nation treaties is *Indian Affairs: Laws and Treaties,* compiled and edited by Charles J. Kappler (Washington: Government Printing Office, 1904, hosted by the Oklahoma State University Library Electronic Publishing Center).

Within the U.S. Constitution, articles I and II grant the U.S. President and the Congress authority to declare war and enter into treaties. The Supremacy Clause contained in article VI, clause two, states that treaties are part of the supreme law of the land. The sovereign-to-sovereign policy era provides context for the frequent treaty-making occurring between the United States and Tribal Nations up until 1871. In that year, the U.S. House of Representatives passed a rider on an appropriations bill meant to curtail the authority of the Senate to approve further treaty-making with Tribes. From 1871 forward, the federal government continued to negotiate with Tribes through executive orders and formal agreements, but no longer labeled them as "treaties."

The historical entry into treaties between Tribal Nations and the United States involved the separate governmental objectives on each side of the treaty. Interpretation of treaties requires discerning the mutual understanding reached within the concluded document. U.S. representatives in regional areas often formulated template treaty documents for land cessions and then added specific language depending on the negotiations with individual tribal leaders. A primary motivation for the United States was to secure land cessions to build a permanent presence in North America to the exclusion of other governments from Europe. Tribal leadership commonly negotiated treaty agreements from a kinship perspective by granting territorial rights to allow for nearby U.S. settlement while maintaining homeland activities in tribal territories. The kinship perspective embodied a belief in taking the U.S. citizens as relatives and employing familial terms to the negotiation process in furtherance of alliance building. These two divergent perspectives continue to impact the significance of treaty documents between Tribal Nations and the United States.

Much has been written on the uneven balance of power through these treaty negotiations due to the template format, the documents written in the English language using legal terminology, the false promises made to obtain signatures or the failure to obtain valid consent from legitimate tribal leadership. In addition, many treaties sent to the U.S. Senate for approval were unilaterally modified without the knowledge of the tribal leadership and approved contrary to the terms consented to. These circumstances surrounding the treaty documents have resulted in special interpretive tools applied by the U.S. judiciary for construing treaty terms. The Indian canons of construction apply to treaty documents and require the following: 1) treaties are to be construed as the Indians would have understood them, 2) any ambiguities are to be construed in favor of the Indian understanding of the treaty document, and 3) all powers and rights are reserved to a Tribe unless expressly relinquished in a treaty document. These interpretative tools have been expanded to also apply to federal statutes and regulations enacted on Indian matters.

The reserved lands of a Tribe are commonly referred to as the tribal reservation. Tribal reservations were formally acknowledged in U.S. law through treaties, executive orders or formal agreements. Tribal territories are often much larger than the current size of tribal reservations. Many Tribal Nations reserved off-reservation access to customary fishing and hunting territories that remain in force today. The totality of tribal land holdings are referred to as "Indian Country," a legal term of art. A more extensive discussion of tribal property is provided in Chapter 2: "American Indian Property Law."

In conclusion, the treaty negotiation was the basis of interaction founding the current relationships between Tribal Nations and the United States. Upon this foundation have been added hundreds of additional agreements between Tribes and the U.S., a variety of federal laws, and many federal regulations involving these relationships. A common feature of the treaty-making foundation is the pledge of alliance and protection from both tribal and federal leadership.

Treaties, formal agreements, compacts and contracts continue to have vitality in the field of federal Indian law and tribal law. These are the primary sources for resolving legal issues between Tribal Nations and the United States. The first step in analyzing a cross-governmental issue involving a Tribal Nation and the U.S. federal or state governments is to review relevant treaties, agreements or other negotiated instruments.

b. Removal Era (1800s)

Following the treaty-making of the sovereign-to-sovereign era, white settlers began encroaching into tribally reserved territories and homelands. Political voices of the time called for removal of all Native Americans from the eastern seaboard to beyond the Appalachian mountain range into lands west of the Mississippi River. Under the administration of President Andrew Jackson, the official policy of the United States government was to remove all Natives west. This policy was memorialized by Congress in the Indian Removal Act of May 28, 1830, 4 Stat. 411. While this Act outlined a voluntary removal policy for Tribes wishing to exchange their homelands for western lands, the policy as implemented by the U.S. military under President Jackson was forcible removal marches of men, women and children where thousands died en route to the new territories.

For example, the Cherokee Nation protested the actions of local state governments and the U.S. federal government in seeking their removal from homelands memorialized in a series of treaties with the U.S. government. Beginning in 1835 with the illegitimate treaty at New Echota signed by a small number of Cherokee removal supporters, the U.S. government exerted military pressure until the summer of 1838 when the forced march known as the "Trail of Tears" occurred with over four thousand people dying along the way to the Indian Territory. Southern Tribal Nations which endured the forced military march policy, included the Seminole, Creek, Chickasaw, Choctaw, and as mentioned previously, the Cherokee Nation.

Numerous Tribal Nations were caught up in the U.S. removal policy from the northern Tribal Nations, such as the Seneca, Onondaga, Tuscarora, Cayuga, Mohawk, Oneida, Potawatomi, Shawnee, and many others. The Potawatomi removal has become known as the "Trail of Death" along the route from present-day Indiana and Illinois to reservations in present-day Kansas and Oklahoma. The routes that Native American people were marched over are recalled in oral and written tribal histories. A single Tribal Nation may have splintered into several different governments as groups of families refused to march further along the removal routes. From these histories, a series of tribal governments have formed for certain formerly consolidated Tribal Nations. For almost every forced tribal removal, a group remained behind in the homelands and some eventually did receive formal federal recognition as independent Tribal Nations.

Wars of resistance to removal efforts were fought during the 1800s by many Tribal Nations lacking the metal weapons and numbers of the U.S. military forces they faced. Between 1866 and 1891, more than one thousand battles were fought between Native peoples and the United States military. When the U.S. military attacked peaceful settlements of unarmed men, women and children, the resulting killing of Native Americans has been labeled massacres by historians. Examples of such massacres, include the Sand Creek Massacre where Cheyenne and Arapaho men, women and children were slaughtered under a flag of truce on November 29, 1864 and the Wounded Knee Massacre of December 29, 1890 where over 300 unarmed men, women, and children on their way to the Pine Ridge Reservation to seek protection were killed by U.S. cavalry. A leading text on the history surrounding many of the wars of Native resistance is Dee Brown's *Bury My Heart at Wounded Knee: An Indian History of the American West* (Henry Holt and Company 1970).

c. Reservation Era (1800s)

Overlapping with the Removal Era was the Reservation Era of U.S. Indian policy. The Reservation Era is treated as a separate policy era due to the extensive re-defining of tribal property boundaries and relationships with the Euro-Americans. During this era, the Bureau of Indian Affairs (BIA) was relocated from the Department of War to the Department of the Interior in 1849. The BIA following federal policy sought to impose control over Native Americans through federal Indian agents located within tribal territories. The lands reserved under treaty and formal agreements known as reservations for tribal peoples had exact boundaries established during this era. From the U.S. policy perspective, separation between Native and white communities was accomplished through the reservation policy. From the Tribal Nations' perspectives, stability and re-structuring opportunities were viewed as the benefits of the reservation era, usually after removal and/or wars of resistance had been fought with the United States.

Many Tribal Nations when relocated to completely new geographical locations became immediately dependent on treaty-guaranteed food and equipment provisions. The BIA was the federal agency charged with carrying out the treaty responsibilities of the U.S. government, such as providing the rations, farming implements, cloth, and other goods agreed upon in the exchanges between Tribes and federal officials. During this time period, the leadership in the BIA began forming a comprehensive agenda to control and re-orient Native Americans into Euro-American norms. Supported by Euro-American theories of superiority and civilization, federal policy started to shift from the idea of neighboring communities to fundamental re-socialization of Native people.

d. Allotment/Assimilation Era (late 1800s to early 1900s)

The devastation and trauma to tribal communities during the Allotment/Assimilation Era cannot be overstated. Through twin goals of breaking up tribal land bases and re-socializing Native peoples to follow Euro-American Christian norms as farmers, the U.S. implemented policies in violation of treaties, formal agreements and promises given to tribal leaders. With Indian agents on reservations dictating food rations and controlling monetary payments under treaties and agreements, the BIA began to implement a policy of social experimentation to convert Native people into the mold of white Christian farmers.

In 1883, the federal Indian Commissioner established the Courts of Indian Offenses as mechanisms that served, at best, for peace and order in tribal territories and at worst, as means to punish the expression of tribal practices and customs. In *U.S. v. Clapox*, 35 F. 575 (1888), the federal district court in Oregon held that those who had rescued a fellow tribal member, Minnie, from the jails of the local Indian agent had violated federal law. Although Minnie was being held on a charge of adultery not listed as any offense under federal statute or the regulations for the Court of Indian Offenses, the federal judge broadly read the treaty with the Umatilla Tribe to allow for the U.S. to punish any behavior categorized as a crime on the reservation. 35 F. at 576–77. Further, the federal judge distinguished the Courts of Indian Offenses from the U.S. courts established under the authority of the U.S. Constitution in Section 1 Article III. Rather, the court's opinion characterized the Courts of Indian Offenses as: "mere educational and disciplinary instrumentalities, by which the government of the United States is endeavoring to improve and elevate the condition of these dependent tribes to whom it sustains the relation of guardian. In fact, the reservation itself is in the nature of a school, and the Indians are gathered there, under the charge of an agent, for the purpose of acquiring the habits, ideas, and aspirations which distinguish the civilized from the uncivilized man." 35 F. at 577. With no limitations on the discretionary authority of Indian agents, Native American adults were punished for all manner of tribal activities from participating in spiritual ceremonies to wearing their hair long to refusing to allow their children to be taken to the government-endorsed boarding schools.

In the late 1800s, the official agenda of BIA leadership was to assimilate Native people into "white civilization." The quickest path to re-socialization of Native Americans was determined to be the mass kidnapping of tribal children and forced attendance in military-style governmental and religious boarding schools. There have been many accounts of heartbroken parents having their crying children, four to eight year-olds usually, seized from their homes and sent long distances to experience often physically, mentally, emotionally, and sexually abusive conditions.

An entire generation of tribal peoples grew up under the brutal conditions of mandatory boarding school education where they were punished for speaking Native languages, for failing to immediately respond to English commands, and for trying to assist other younger children being punished at the hands of governmental officials, nuns, priests, and other religious leaders. Members of this generation have described the ultimate consequences of the government-endorsed boarding schools as: disruption of tribal family structures, loss of Native languages, an epidemic of alcoholism and drug abuse in Indian Country, intergenerational abuse towards children, and a sense of isolation from both tribal and white communities that led in many instances to high rates of suicide.

In addition to the social experimentation on Native peoples individually, formal U.S. Indian policy focused on the tribal land base in communal ownership as an impediment to the goal of civilizing the Tribal Nations. A catalyst to these federal policies was Henry Dawes. As a member of Congress, Dawes introduced a rider on a federal appropriations bill in 1871 to end treaty-making with Tribal Nations. After that date, the U.S. continued to enter into formal agreements and recognize reservations through federal legislation and the executive authority of the U.S. president. As a Senator, Henry Dawes secured a position on the Senate Indian Affairs Committee and sponsored federal legislation to parcel out the communal tribal land bases to individual tribal members, thereby "freeing up" lands for continued white settlement. This legislation was formerly titled, the General Allotment Act of 1887, 25 U.S.C. § 331, and is commonly referred to as the "Dawes Act."

One of the processes established through implementation of the Dawes Act was the drawing up by federal officials of formal tribal rolls to determine who would be entitled to a parcel of land, an allotment. The federally-created tribal rolls would have a lasting impact on designating those who were counted as citizens of a Tribal Nation. Mistakes made in the process were memorialized in the federal rolls and would impact all descendants of that tribal member, family or group. Anecdotal accounts of Indian agents purposefully excluding "troublesome" tribal members from the rolls exists. Tribal peoples were also given English interpretations of their names or wholly renamed in the process by federal officials. In the next time period, the federal tribal membership rolls became further solidified as the starting point for tribal citizenship when written into tribal constitutions. Another extension of federal authority over tribal citizens was embodied in the Indian Citizenship Act of 1924, 43 Stat. 253 Act of June 2, 1924, where U.S. citizenship was extended over all tribal peoples and created dual citizenship in the U.S. and specific Tribal Nations.

With completion of the tribal rolls, Indian agents either selected an allotment within the reservation boundaries or requested the tribal member select an allotment. For example, a tribal member may have selected an allotment where family members had been laid to rest to prevent the land from leaving the family. As the family cemetery area, the tribal member would then flout the wishes of the agent by refusing to till the land for farming purposes. Accounts exist of the best farming lands being excluded from the available areas tribal members were allowed to pick from. The practical results of the allotment policy were the allotment of the tribal lands from communal to private ownership; the transfer of the unallotted lands to the U.S. government at a price it set; destruction of the seasonal harvesting and rotation within the tribal territory due to the private property boundaries from allotments; influx of white settlers into the tribal territory through purchasing title from the U.S. government; and the loss of over 27 million acres.

> Between 1887 and 1934, the tribal lands of 118 reservations were allotted, although many reservations, particularly in the Southwest, escaped allotment. From 1887 to 1900, the federal government approved 53,168 allotments, totaling nearly 5 million acres, and almost 36 million acres were allotted by 1920. By 1934, approximately 27 million acres, or two-thirds of all the land allotted to tribal members, had passed by sale or involuntary transfer from the Indian fee owner into non-Indian ownership. *Cohen's Handbook of Federal Indian Law,* § 16.03[2][b], (Lexis Nexis 2012 edition).

Without the tribal territory as a resource for harvesting and hunting, entire Tribes became impoverished in a short amount of time and completely dependent on federal rations for survival.

Furthermore, the loss of lands within reservation borders has significantly altered tribal jurisdiction and management of the tribal homelands reserved by Tribal Nations for the continued livelihood of tribal citizens.

The dire poverty experienced by the majority of Native Americans during this time period gained federal attention by the 1920s. In response to the conditions on Indian reservations, Secretary of the Interior Hubert Work requested that Lewis Meriam preside over a committee to report on the conditions for Native Americans. Commonly known as the "Meriam Report," the findings submitted to Secretary Work on Feb. 21, 1928 described a depressing state of impoverishment for American Indians. In Chapter One of the report, the first sentence stated: "An overwhelming majority of the Indians are poor, even extremely poor, and they are not adjusted to the economic and social system of the dominant white civilization." The Meriam Report also identified the federal government past policies towards tribal peoples as largely creating the poverty conditions described.

e. Indian Self-Government Era (1930s to 1940s)

Following the Meriam Report, federal policy again shifted with key federal officials in the Department of the Interior seeking to include Native Americans into the "New Deal" policies of the 1930s. With Indian Commissioner John Collier advocating for federal legislation to halt the allotment process and provide for re-structuring of tribal governments, the new policy era of Indian self-government was embodied in the Indian Reorganization Act (IRA) of 1934, 25 U.S.C. §§ 461–479. The details of Collier's legislative proposal and the eventual enactment of the compromise IRA by Congress are carefully set forth in Vine Deloria, Jr. and Clifford M. Lytle's book, *The Nations Within: The Past and Future of American Indian Sovereignty* (University of Texas Press 1998).

Several significant features of the IRA changed the political and economic landscape for Tribal Nations. The first provision of the IRA ended the policy of allotment for American Indian lands, 25 U.S.C. § 461. The second provision indefinitely extended the trust status of Indian lands held by the U.S. government as trustee, 25 U.S.C. § 462. With the trust status extended and allotment halted, the IRA also provided for the restoration of lands to tribal ownership and purchase by the Secretary of lands for the benefit of Indians, 25 U.S.C. §§ 463 and 465. Under the IRA, the Secretary of the Interior was granted the authority to establish new Indian reservations and to add lands to existing reservations, 25 U.S.C. § 467.

Other key provisions focused on the reorganization of tribal government into a semblance of the U.S. three branch system under a constitution. The IRA provided that Indian groups were allowed to organize under a tribal constitution as approved by the Secretary of the Interior, 25 U.S.C. § 476(a). Indian agents circulated templates of tribal constitutions for adoption by tribal citizens. The boilerplate constitutions enshrined the standard of tribal membership as based upon the federal tribal rolls with blood quantum requirements for all future members. Often these constitutions contained limits on tribal governmental authority in the form of requiring the U.S. Secretary of the Interior to approve of tribal actions before funding would be released from the U.S. Treasury accounts of the Tribes. On the positive side, the tribal constitutions authorized tribally elected officials to oversee the affairs and resources of the Tribal Nations, loosening the hold of the Indian agents on tribal resources.

With federal recognition of tribal government authority, the Tribal Nations were also empowered under the IRA to establish corporate charters under federal law to manage tribal economic operations, 25 U.S.C. § 477. This shift in federal policy signaled a return to the commercial interaction of historic times between Tribal Nations and the U.S. To further the economic rebuilding of tribal commerce, the IRA instituted a tribal revolving loan fund for Indian chartered corporations,25 U.S.C. § 470. However, at this point in history, the U.S. had established itself as the trustee over tribal resources and thereby, limited the negotiating, contracting or maximizing of tribal commercial activity.

In spite of the intergenerational poverty of tribal communities, many Tribal Nations reorganized under federally-approved tribal constitutions. Those who rejected the IRA constitutions also benefitted from the federal policy shift in re-establishing economic activity and greater control over the future of tribal communities. As the tides turned and tribal governments regained some of their former strength, moderate economic activity began to return on a foundational level for a significant number of tribal communities.

f. Termination Era (1940s to 1960s)

As tribal communities began to pursue economic development under the IRA incentives, anti-tribal forces sought to stymie tribal governmental authority; end the separate landholdings of tribal government and citizens; and assert state jurisdiction over tribal territories. Representing state interests in the federal government, U.S. Congress members responded to these political forces by stating the official federal policy as terminating federal recognition of certain Tribal Nations and placing tribal citizens exclusively under the laws of the United States with House Resolution No. 108, 83rd Congress (August 1, 1953). Under the termination policy, over one hundred Tribal Nations were terminated from federal recognition. Tribal lands were auctioned off or parceled out, losing their tribal character under federal law. Resources and assets were sold with payments divided between those on the tribal rolls. Termination of federal recognition disqualified tribal citizens from receiving treaty-guaranteed services in health, education, or training programs.

This policy era galvanized tribal leadership nationally to establish formal associations to address federal policymakers and voice tribal perspectives on legislation directed their way. The National Congress of American Indians was founded in 1944 and regional tribal leadership organizations emerged across the country. The termination era was diametrically opposed to the prior era of Indian self-government. Instead of negotiating with Tribal Nations under federal policy, the U.S. policy had switched to refusing to recognize the existence of specific Tribal Nations as governments with citizens.

Programs implemented to hasten the termination policy included the urban relocation program and the delegation of federal criminal jurisdiction to states in tribal communities. The 1952 Urban Indian Relocation Program brought hundreds of Native Americans from rural reservation communities to heavily populated, industrialized major cities in the United States. The program promised relocatees temporary housing, guidance and job counseling by the BIA in initially seven cities: Chicago, Denver, Los Angeles, San Francisco, San Jose, St. Louis, Cincinnati, Cleveland, and Dallas. An estimated 750,000 tribal citizens relocated during this time to urban areas, but many returned to tribal communities after the promises of the BIA went unfulfilled and a sense of alienation set in at the new urban locations.

A second thrust of the termination era was the enactment of Public Law 280, providing a delegation of federal criminal jurisdiction to states. This extension of state jurisdiction over tribal communities did not require tribal consent until 1968. Due to the often strained relationships between state government and tribal governments, the delegation to state authority was often unwelcome from the tribal perspective. This law and its implications will be more fully explored in Chapter 3: "Criminal Jurisdiction in Indian Country."

In sum, the termination era was a reversal of the prior policy era empowering tribal governments to rebuild economically and politically. To many, the federal policy of termination was viewed as an injustice to Native Americans. Through the urban relocation program, many tribal citizens became familiar with political movements emerging in the 1960s. In the late 1960s, new tribal voices emerged from reservations and urban areas in opposition to the termination policy and past U.S. policies negatively impacting Tribes.

g. Indian Self-Determination Era (late 1960s to present)

With the U.S. nationally focused on the civil rights movement in the 1960s, urban Indians were inspired to arrange protest activities against the federal control over tribal communities and the termination policy. In response to the national attention being garnered by American Indians in protest of the termination policy, U.S. President Richard Nixon delivered a "Special Message on Indian Affairs" to the U.S. Congress on July 8, 1970. President Nixon called the forced termination policy wrong in his message and called upon Congress to encourage Indian self-determination. One of the seminal pieces of legislation enacted heralding in the new federal policy was the Indian Self-Determination and Education Assistance Act of 1975, 25 U.S.C. § 450. This statute and others enacted since have encouraged tribal government administration of services to tribal citizens with the intention of lessening BIA control over tribal communities. The current era of U.S. Indian policy remains the Indian self-determination era and will be more fully discussed in later chapters.

2. Federal Statutes, Federal Agencies, and Federal Regulations in Federal Indian Law

By virtue of the Indian Commerce Clause, the U.S. Congress is empowered within the federal government to regulate Indian affairs. The impact of federal legislation on the lives of tribal citizens cannot be overstated. Federal Indian laws and policies have redefined tribal property rights, tribal education, tribal health services, tribal law enforcement, tribal economics, tribal civil and criminal jurisdiction, and many other major aspects of tribal society and governance. As the U.S. judiciary broadly defined congressional authority over Tribes as "plenary authority" stemming from political relationships and based on the Indian Commerce Clause, the U.S. Congress has passed legislation touching nearly every facet of tribal life. Federal statutes form a large portion of federal Indian law and will be extensively discussed throughout this text. Title 25 of the United States Code is entirely composed of federal laws regarding American Indian people.

Under the U.S. executive power are the federal administrative agencies that implement federal legislation and policy. In 1824, the U.S. Bureau of Indian Affairs (BIA) was established within the Department of War and in 1849 was transferred to the Department of the Interior. The BIA has primary responsibility to implement federal Indian law and policy; to deliver treaty-guaranteed services; and to administer the daily trust management functions of the federal government to Tribal Nations and tribal citizens. The BIA has its headquarters in Washington, D.C., operates twelve regional offices, and various area offices located directly in Indian Country. A wide-range of tribal programs are overseen and administered through the BIA including: tribal education, tribal economic development, tribal law enforcement, and tribal court services. Federal funding for tribal services flow through the BIA to Tribal Nations for these programs based upon treaty entitlements, self-determination contracts and self-governance contracts in the interest of restoring the quality of life to tribal citizenry after the devastating federal policies of the 1800s.

Supplementing the BIA provision of federal services are other federal agencies interacting with tribal governments. The Indian Health Service (IHS), originally within the Department of the Interior, operates from the Department of Health and Human Services to provide healthcare to American Indians and Alaska Natives. Another specialized agency is the Office of Special Trustee (OST) created in 1994 under the American Indian Trust Fund Management and Reform Act within the Department of the Interior. The OST implements the fiduciary responsibilities for tribal beneficiaries owning tribal lands in federal trust status.

Other federal agencies, such as the Bureau of Land Management (BLM) and the Department of Housing and Urban Development (HUD), may administer specific federal programs intended for tribal governments and tribal citizens within their overall responsibilities. By Presidential Executive Order No. 13175 Consultation and Coordination with Tribal Governments (November 6, 2000) and Presidential Memorandum, Tribal Consultation (November 5, 2009), federal agencies have been directed to provide meaningful consultation and collaboration with tribal governments prior to taking action which will significantly implicate tribal interests. The directive to consult with tribal governments to federal agencies has led to more tribal leadership input into the federal decision-making process where tribal interests are affected.

Due to the broad involvement of federal agencies in relationship with tribal governments, regulations promulgated by such federal agencies are important in federal Indian law. Administrative law principles are applicable when federal regulations involving federal Indian law are being construed. Additionally, the aforementioned Indian canons of construction apply with equal force to federal statutes and federal regulations involving tribal interests. Thus, ambiguities in federal Indian laws and regulations are to be interpreted in favor of Indian interests.

3. Federal Court Decisions: Key Role in Federal Indian Law

The U.S. Supreme Court has taken a leading role in the development of federal Indian law since the beginning of the federal judiciary. Most scholars view the foundation of federal Indian law as defined by three U.S. Supreme Court opinions penned by Chief Justice John Marshall in the early 1800s, known as the Marshall Trilogy. The first of the three, *Johnson v. McIntosh* (21 U.S. (8Wheat) 543, 1823), set forth a limitation on tribal property rights based on the international concept of the doctrine of discovery. The opinion held that Indians had a right of occupancy to Indian lands and the discovering European nation held superior title to those same lands. The United States as successor to Great Britain had thus obtained superior title to all Indian lands in mid-North America and limited the ability of Indians to sell their lands to any purchaser except the United States according to this court decision.

The second and third cases in the Marshall Trilogy involved the resistance of the Cherokee Nation to the adverse actions of the state of Georgia. In *Cherokee Nation v. Georgia* (30 U.S. (5 Pet.) 1, 1831), an injunction was sought against implementation of Georgia state laws asserting ownership and authority over Cherokee Nation lands and jurisdiction in contravention of tribal sovereignty and treaties with the United States. The U.S. Supreme Court opined that the Cherokee Nation was not a foreign nation with standing to bring a lawsuit under Article III section two of the U.S. Constitution. Rather, the Court found that the Cherokee Nation was a "domestic dependent nation," a new political term created by the Court which did not entitle the Tribe to sue in federal court. The Court also stated that there existed a ward/guardian relationship between the Tribal Nation and the United States, but went on to dismiss the case due to a lack of standing to appear before the Court.

The third case involved the laws of Georgia in Cherokee Nation lands as imposed upon Samuel Worcester, a missionary under the protection of the federal government. In *Worcester v. Georgia* (31 U.S. (6 Pet.) 515, 1832), a habeas petition was brought by Mr. Worcester when he was incarcerated by Georgia officials for failing to obtain state permissions and swear an oath to the state prior to entering Cherokee lands. This case afforded Chief Justice John Marshall the ability to provide a detailed account of the relationships between the United States and tribal governments based upon the sovereign-to-sovereign era. The Court held in the case that federal law preempted state law in Indian affairs upholding the treaty relationship between the United States and the Cherokee Nation and voiding the Georgia laws in contravention of treaty provisions. Thus, the Marshall Trilogy has served as a foundation for federal Indian law in imposing limits on tribal property rights, redefining tribal governments as "domestic dependent nations" in a "ward/guardian" relationship with the United States, and establishing federal preemption over state laws in Indian affairs.

U.S. Supreme Court decisions have been pivotal in controversies involving tribal treaty rights, tribal jurisdiction, tribal land rights, and many other major aspects of tribal concern. The U.S. federal judicial system is composed of eleven regional circuits each with district and appellate level courts. Federal courts regularly decide important issues on tribal government and tribal citizen interests. Legal doctrines developed through federal judicial decisions have solidified into federal Indian law principles with significance for tribal litigants. In many instances, cases that have significant impact on tribal rights have advanced in controversies between non-Indian parties where the Tribes where never permitted to make arguments for the Courts or otherwise have their perspectives considered. Many Indian law scholars have criticized the broad authority of the federal judiciary to pronounce new legal doctrines in federal Indian law that lack textual support in the U.S. Constitution or other written sources of federal law. The federal judiciary has played and continues to play a key role in the formation of federal Indian law.

Checkpoints

- American Indian Law originated from concepts developed in international law. The interaction between tribal governments and the U.S. developed through the treaty-making process.

- There are over 560 federally-recognized tribal governments in the United States. Each Tribe has its own governance structure and set of tribal laws.

- Federal Indian law is applied generally to all Tribes whether enacted by federal legislation or through a federal judicial opinion. Title 25 of the U.S. Code contains the set of federal laws dealing with American Indians. Federal agencies implement many of the federal Indian law provisions. The Bureau of Indian Affairs has a primary role in implementing federal Indian law and policy.

- The Marshall Trilogy of cases serve as the foundation of the relationship between tribal governments and the U.S. Key concepts from the cases include: tribal governments characterized as "domestic dependent nations," the U.S. as the successor to the discovery doctrine from Great Britain, the beginning of the federal trust relationship from the "ward/guardian" status, and federal preemption of state law in Indian affairs.

Chapter 2

American Indian Property Law

Roadmap

- Understand that tribal property systems were diverse and existed prior to European contact and were based on family, clan and individual ownership and use concepts, depending on the community.

- Learn that the international "Doctrine of Discovery" was employed by the U.S. Supreme Court to transform tribal property rights into rights of occupancy. To acquire Indian property rights, U.S. federal Indian law requires purchase or conquest to change the land status to U.S. title.

- Learn that tribal property rights were fundamentally changed by federal law through the General Allotment Act of 1887 and other tribally specific allotment legislation. These federal laws dramatically reduced the reserved tribal land base and provided the means for federal agents to allot reserved tribal lands into small parcels in individual tribal ownership. These allotments are held in trust status for the Indian owners by the U.S.

- Learn that the status of tribal land as either held in trust by the U.S. government or as owned in fee simple title has legal implications on whether the tribal government has primary regulatory authority or whether a state government may have types of regulatory authority as caselaw has developed in federal Indian law.

- Know that federal Indian law restricts the sale, lease and other encumbrances of Indian land, so that only the U.S. government can purchase any Indian lands with clear title due to the Non-Intercourse Acts.

- Know that after the loss of millions of acres of land through dealings with the U.S. government, tribal governments and citizens continue to own over 55 million acres of land in trust status.

This chapter will provide an overview of the historical and contemporary property and land tenure systems of American Indian Tribes. Because most every other aspect of American Indian law, from criminal jurisdiction to taxation to business transactions, will turn on the status of the land where a particular activity occurred, it is particularly important to have an understanding of the different forms of property ownership that exist inside Indian country.

A. Historical Context

1. Prior to Colonization

Prior to European contact, Indians had systems of law for recognizing and enforcing property rights. Property rights and dominion over lands existed in varying contexts and tribal communities regulated land use by custom and norms.

History texts often over-generalize and stereotype Indian property by suggesting that Indians did not understand the concept of property ownership. These texts, if they acknowledge any tribal property system at all, restrict tribal "ownership" to one form: a pure "common use" system where every individual or family within a Tribe was free to use lands and natural resources, and that such land use was temporary in nature.

It is doubtful that many Tribes actually practiced a pure form of common ownership as the mainstream history texts describe. Scholars in the last few decades have demonstrated that the historical record departs significantly from the accepted narrative of the mainstream. Tribal communities, particularly those that lived within the same territories for generations, would not have escaped the tragedy of the commons that led to property laws and controls elsewhere throughout the globe. The "tragedy of the commons" is the idea that complete freedom for all to use common areas will result in ruining the resource, therefore some type of property use rules must apply to properly steward resources.

It would have been much more common for either the tribal government, community, clan or family, or individual to exert ownership or property rights in the land to ensure adequate land use over time. This would have translated to land and natural resources such as water, particularly in times of resource scarcity.

There is evidence that most Tribes had some form of recognized ownership and/regulatory control over land, and in many instances, Tribes had elaborate land tenure structures over multiple generations. For example, the Pueblos of the Southwest, the Tribes of the Southeastern United States, and the Iroquois are very well-documented as having elaborate property schemes around agriculture.

It is well documented that some tribal property systems provided government protection to individual property rights that could pass during life and at death. In the Cherokee land tenure system, as consistent with nations around the globe today, individuals could freely acquire and transfer surface rights, including the improvements thereon, but the underlying estates were held by the sovereign, which possessed reversionary interest should private property rights cease by operation of law.

2. Early European/International Law

When Europeans arrived in the Western hemisphere they discovered the American Indian as a pre-existing property owner. Although there was a tendency to marginalize the nature of Indian ownership and dominion over lands, international law recognized that Indians had property rights that could not simply be ignored by the colonizing country. International law's "Doctrine of Discovery" governed the relationships between the various European powers and governed how European powers would interact with one another as they sought to acquire ownership in tribal lands. From the European perspective, tribal lands could either be purchased or taken as the spoils of a "just war."

European sovereigns could not simply declare and perfect absolute ownership over tribal lands without the consent or knowledge of the Tribe in possession of those lands. An affirmative extinguishment of tribal title property rights was first necessary in order to clear title for future ownership by a non-Indian sovereign or individual. "Discovery" merely gave the colonizing country a superior right to acquire lands from the Indians in the future.

The early treaties between European powers and Indian Tribes reflect the understanding that Indians exercised ownership and dominion over lands and that European powers lacked the basic powers over land that are consistent with property ownership.

European powers were the grantees who acquired their property interest through treaty conveyances from the Tribes. The very terms of these early treaties recognize that the Indians, as the grantor, were the party with the power to cede, transfer or convey lands to others.

When one European power became the successor in interest to the previous sovereign, as did the United States after the American Revolution, title or ownership to all lands within the newly claimed boundaries did not automatically pass to the new sovereign. The new sovereign simply stepped into the shoes of the old sovereign and acquired the exclusive right among European powers to acquire lands in the future.

3. Early U.S. Law

The newly independent United States acknowledged Indian dominion over lands in its first Indian property legislation—the Trade and Intercourse Act of 1790—and in numerous treaties whereby Tribes gave permission to federal troops to cross Indian lands. Other treaties involved the outright purchase of lands from the Tribes.

In passing the first legislation dealing with Indian property, the United States did not assert title to all Indian lands but instead, the Trade and Intercourse Act made it unlawful for non-Indian individuals or the states to acquire lands directly from Tribes. Rather, it preserved the exclusive right of the United States to approach Tribes for land conveyances, session, rights of ways or other property transfers. Although the early United States leaders marginalized the nature and extent of tribal property ownership, the body of legislation that followed institutionalized the notion that the United States needed to acquire or extinguish property rights from Indians before the United States could "own" land without a cloud on the title.

As a practical reality, prior and after the passage of the Non-Intercourse acts, individual Indians and landed colonies had frequently purchased lands directly from Tribes or individual Indians. This created a series of conflicts over competing chains of title where the Indians were the grantors and several grantees later claimed that their property rights originated from Indian conveyances.

The United States Supreme Court took this issue up in *Johnson v. M'Intosh*, 21 U.S. (8 Wheat) 543 (1823), where two competing parties sought a judicial determination of property rights. One party produced a chain of title originating directly with an Indian Tribe where the successor in interest from the Tribe was a private individual. One party produced a chain of title originating directly with an Indian Tribe where the successor in interest was the United States. The United States purported to have acquired the same lands from the same Tribe via an armistice treaty after the Tribe had purportedly transferred the land to a private individual.

In reaching the decision that the chain of title involving the United States resulted in superior title, the United States Supreme Court set a precedent that diminished the relative property interests of all Indian Tribes. Rather than recognizing that Tribes, as the original landholders, held fee simple ownership in their lands, the Court defined the Indian property interest as similar to a right of occupancy. And, although the Tribes necessarily retained the power to convey that limited property interest to others, only tribal conveyances to the

United States would be recognized under federal law. In other words, only the United States has the power to extinguish "Indian title."

The Court justified the decision, in part, on the previously mentioned narratives and racial stereotypes of Indians, as an ethnic group that did not use the land efficiently enough to be considered property owners to the same extent as their European counterparts. Justice Marshall wrote:

> We will not enter into the controversy, whether agriculturists, merchants, and manufacturers, have a right, on abstract principles, to expel hunters from the territory they possess, or to contract their limits. But the tribes of Indians inhabiting this country were fierce savages ... whose subsistence was chiefly drawn from the forest. To leave them in possession of their country, was to leave the country a wilderness.... 21 U.S. at 588, 590.

Whether disingenuous or not, two narratives in the Court's opinion served as justification to pave the way for westward expansion and made it easier for the federal government to quickly acquire Indian lands for future redistribution to non-Indian settlers. First, Indian property rights were inferior to non-Indian property rights. Second, Indian land uses were less efficient, and therefore inferior to, non-Indian land uses.

4. Indian or Aboriginal Title

The chain of title for most lands within the United States begins with the extinguishment of Indian title followed by subsequent redistribution from the federal government to an individual or entity, either by purchase or land grants. Although largely an historical footnote, there are modern day consequences where tribal lands were acquired by colonies, states or individuals without proper extinguishment of Indian property interests, and cloud on the title may remain.

Most of the situations where lands were acquired in violation of the Trade and Intercourse Acts have been addressed through court cases and/or various legislative acts passed for the purposes of settling any outstanding land claims that could prevent the passage of clear title in the current real estate market. It is possible, however, in researching the land transactions for a given tract of land to find unresolved Indian title issues that may impact the ability to freely alienate lands once held by Tribes.

5. Recognized Title

Although original Indian title was deemed to be limited to an occupancy right or possessory interest in lands, other more complete Indian property interest followed. Once the United States affirmatively recognizes an Indian property right in specified lands, the federal government cannot take the property without compensation. The "recognition" of such a property right may be found in a treaty or statutory provision, or in a deed and land patent. Where there is no clear evidence that the United States "recognized" Indian title to land, the Tribe is not entitled to compensation for takings as a matter of law.

The story of Paha Sapa, the Black Hills of the Great Sioux Nation, highlights the problem, from a tribal perspective, of a federal system that acknowledges tribal ownership of lands on one hand, but then empowers a system where Tribes can be disposed of those lands without their consent.

The tribes at issue have spent two centuries fighting for the return of their sacred Black Hills after they have been dispossessed from lands that hold not just property rights, but religious, cultural and political significance. The wars of the 1860s were fought by the Sioux to protect the integrity of earlier recognized treaty lands from incursions from non-Indian settlers. At the conclusion of those battles, the terms of the Treaty of Fort Laramie constituted recognized title in which the United States acknowledged the future property rights of the Tribes to the exclusion of non-Indians. "Recognized title" included the Black Hills which were later transferred into non-Indian ownership in a series of transactions intended to open the lands for mining purposes.

The U.S. Supreme Court in *United States v. Sioux Nation*, 448 U.S. 371 (1980), ruled that the dispossession of Paha Sapa was an uncompensated taking of tribal property rights by the United States. The judicial remedy available to the Sioux Nation is limited — the only remedy for the taking of the lands is monetary, based on the value of the land at the time of the taking. The Sioux are entitled to a money judgment but are not entitled under federal law, to a return of the lands.

Recognized title is superior to Indian or aboriginal title in a hierarchy of land ownership structures. As the Sioux example best describes, it provides inadequate protections when the United States disregards the will of the Tribe as property owner and acts without tribal consent, or in this case, over the express objection of the Tribe.

That fact that Tribes receive compensation does not soften the effect, from the tribal perspective, of repeated actions by the federal government to invoke a large scale compulsory purchase system for the purpose of removing Indians from lands wanted for non-Indian settlement.

The most common story known to the mainstream audience of dispossession of Indian lands is likely the Cherokee Trail of Tears, a forced removal of the Cherokee people from their lands in the southeastern United States to lands within present-day northeastern Oklahoma. Almost every Tribe has endured a similar relocation.

After the Tribes were relocated to a new or modified land base, new treaties once again recognized Indian property ownership. Typically, the tribal government was recognized as being the beneficial owner on behalf of the people. In some circumstances, lands were conveyed to the Tribes in fee simple absolute as a single large contiguous land base.

During the immediate post-removal period, most Tribes held their lands in common in a contiguous land base where non-Indian ownership of lands was prohibited. In fact, it was the preference of the federal government that the Tribe as a whole, and not individual Indians, hold the land. If any further land cessions were to be acquired from the Indians, it was much easier to have a single transaction with the tribal government than to recognize, as a matter of federal law, that individual Indians had property rights. In fact, where tribal law unequivocally recognized and protected individual property interests, the federal government ignored those laws.

The continued desire for Indian land for non-Indian settlement soon ushered in a new federal Indian policy as set forth in the General Allotment Act of 1887, codified at 25 U.S.C. § 331 (repealed).

B. Allotment Process

The General Allotment Act was not self-executing and did not apply to all Tribes. A few Tribes were successful in avoiding allotment and continue to maintain contiguous land bases where they retain the right to exclude non-Indian ownership to this day.

Where allotment occurred, it was the result of tribally-specific agreements, generally under duress, or a result of unilateral federal action to allot lands even over tribal objection. Therefore, allotment occurred in different ways, and depending on the reservation or territory, one must research the tribal specific laws that give rise to the modern day land tenure system within each tribal territory.

The federal allotment policy of the late nineteenth century, which converted the tribal land base into small parcels of individually-owned property, has rendered most tribal economies unviable. The effects of the allotment policy, although long refuted, continue to limit economic development for both private endeavors of individual Indians and sustainability of tribal economies.

The allotment policy, as a social experiment, was designed to assimilate individual Indians into mainstream American society. Through the allotment policy, as an economic and property experiment, individual Indians were to be transformed into owners of privately held lands subject to the United States property law system, to the exclusion of on-going tribal involvement.

Proponents of allotment convinced Congress that Indians did not understand or value individual property rights. Allotment would ideally teach Indians the importance of individual property rights to better prepare them for United States citizenship. In fact for many Tribes, acceptance of an allotment was coupled with immediate U.S. naturalized citizenship, tribal people at that point being exclusive citizens of their tribal nation.

Although a growing number of contemporary scholars have refuted the notion of tribal communal ownership by providing evidence of extensive private property rights at tribal law, the federal government simply disregarded the existence of tribal property laws that were in effect at the time of allotment. The federal government also ignored the opposition of Indian people who were content with tribal property law regimes. In doing so, the rights of the individual Indians which were otherwise protected under tribal law were ignored to make way for the forced federal allotment of tribal lands. Sometimes, allotment deeds actually reduced the land holdings of individual Indians, as evidenced by the testimony of an Indian farmer:

> Under our old Cherokee regime I spent the early days of my life on the farm up here of 300 acres, and arranged to be comfortable in my old age.... When I was assigned to that 60 acres, and I could take no more under the inexorable law of allotment enforced upon us Cherokees, I had to relinquish every inch of my premises outside of that little 60 acres.... What am I going to do with it? For the last few years.... I have gone out there on that farm day after day.... I have exerted all my ability, all industry, all my intelligence ... to make my living out of that 60 acres, and, God be my judge, I have not been able to do it.... I am here to-day [sic], a poor man upon the verge of starvation — my muscular energy gone, hope gone. I have nothing to charge my calamity to but the unwise legislation of Congress in reference to my Cherokee people.
> D.W.C. Duncan, How Allotment Impoverishes the Indians: Testimony Before a Senate Comm. Investigating Conditions in the Indian Territory, November 1906, in GREAT DOCUMENTS IN AMERICAN INDIAN HISTORY 287–88 (Wayne Moquin with Charles Van Doren eds., 1973).

Once an individual allotment was conveyed to the individual allottee, the land was then governed by Anglo-American property law, most often federal law but in some instances, the laws of the surrounding state.

In addition to creating highly fractionated estates where the following generations would inherit smaller and smaller interests in a finite land base, the allotment process resulted in a catastrophic loss of tribal land. Estimates suggest that by 1934, the allotment process resulted in the loss of 86 million acres to non-Indian ownership, either individual private or state/federal public lands. Other estimates suggest that by the end of the allotment era, two-thirds of all the land allotted passed out of Indian ownership.

The proponents of the allotment policy thought it was in the best interest of the Tribes to abandon all forms of common ownership in favor of individual property rights. It was believed, or at least stated, that common tribal ownership was stagnating any chance for economic or social development in Indian country.

The allotment policy was firmly rooted in the notion that farming and other agricultural pursuits were the best use for land. Common lands should be divided into individual parcels so that the individual Indian could become a farmer with the incentive to work harder and make the most profit from his land. The policy ignored that many individual Indians had been farmers for many generations and that those Indian agriculturalists held individual title, under tribal law, to lands they had already improved.

The tribal governments were never compensated for the loss of government ownership even when the transactions violated express treaty guarantees. The federal action of allotting lands without tribal consent, and in express violation of treaty guarantees, was unsuccessfully challenged in the federal courts during the allotment era. In *Lone Wolf v. Hitchcock*, 187 U.S. 553 (1903),the U.S. Supreme Court upheld the authority of the U.S. Congress to allot lands without tribal consent even if the action violated treaty provisions. Further, the tribal governments were not entitled to compensation because the transaction was viewed, not as a taking, but as an appropriate exercise of federal administrative power over tribal property, even when the Tribe owned the lands in fee simple absolute.

> In effect, the action of Congress now complained of was but an exercise of such power, a mere change in the form of investment of Indian tribal property, the property of those who ... were in substantial effect the wards of the government. We must presume that Congress acted in perfect good faith in the dealings with the Indians ... and that the legislative branch of the government exercised its best judgment in the premises. 187 U.S. at 568.

The allotment of tribal lands eventually led to the loss of most of the land that was still under tribal control at the end of the late nineteenth century. Ninety percent of the land owned by Indians at the time of European contact had already been taken before the allotment process ever began.

The loss of land continued, and in fact rapidly increased, following allotment. One reason for rapid loss of land is that once the lands were parceled out to individual Indians, those lands were no longer under the watchful protection of either the federal government or the tribal government. Individual lands were freely alienable and could be acquired by state eminent domain or by adverse possession. The lands became subject to state debtor-creditor laws and forced sales for failure to pay state taxes. Prior to allotment, only the federal government could acquire Indian lands. After allotment, Indian lands could be acquired through private transactions like any other piece of land. The land transactions that followed almost always resulted in the land passing, once and for all, to non-Indians.

After allotments were made to those on the tribal rolls, there were often significant parcels of land remaining. These lands were deemed "surplus" because it was presumed that the Tribe didn't need the land, or implicitly, that the Tribe wouldn't make good use of the lands. If a future tribal use for the lands could be contemplated, there were other people who could make better uses of the land: the white settlers who the federal government had previously promised to keep away from Indian land.

In fact, white homesteaders acquired 60 million acres of the Indian land through this federally sanctioned program. Although Tribes received some compensation for the surplus lands, their consent was irrelevant. After tribal land was acquired by the United States, the "surplus" lands were typically returned to the public domain, making way for homestead deeds to non-Indian private landowners.

C. The Impact of Allotment

Today, the allotted lands that remain under Indian control are typically highly fractionated with multiple co-owners sharing the same parcel of land deeded to a common ancestor. There was no foresight for dealing with these issues, because the allotment policy was designed to end tribal governance and tribal community life.

The allotment process was intended to prepare the Indians for ultimate United States citizenship and full inclusion into the American melting pot. When that did not happen, the practical problems with allotment were quickly revealed and those problems have been exasperated with each passing generation.

On a positive note, Congress quickly repudiated the federal policy of land allotment when it passed the Indian Reorganization Act of 1934. Although the legislation is best known and more often cited for provisions which recognized the rights of Tribes to pass their own constitutions and move toward self-government, the legislation contained property provisions that ended the allotment process. Lands that were still held in trust by the federal government for an allottee in 1934 had the trust periods indefinitely extended so that the lands remained inalienable, 25 U.S.C. § 462. Although there continue to be considerable problems with land fractionation and trust administration, lands have not passed out of Indian hands as a result of the Indian Reorganization Act's extension of the trust period.

Much of the problems associated with the administration of trust lands come from the number of co-owners that frequently exist on a single tract of land. When an original allottee dies without proper estate planning, their property interest will pass, in intestate succession, equally to all of their children. With each generation, the number of co-owners increases, yet the tribal land base can never expand because it is locked into a finite number of parcels. As the number of co-owners increase, the property interest of each co-owner is diminished and the more difficult it becomes to make efficient use of the land.

Congress has recognized that highly fractionated allotments preclude any meaningful economic development in Indian country. The allotment process that was premised on maximizing the efficiency of Indian land use has rendered most Indian land useless. There are multiple examples that illustrate the problem of fractionated ownership in Indian country but the most famous description follows:

> Tract 1305 is 40 acres and produces $1,080 in income annually. It is valued at $8,000. It has 439 owners, one-third of whom receive less than $.05 in annual rent and two-thirds of whom receive less than $1.... The common denominator used to compute fractional interests in the property is [3 trillion, 394 billion, 923 million, 840 thousand.] The smallest heir receives $.01 every 177 years ... The administrative costs of handling this tract are estimated by the Bureau of Indian Affairs at $17,560 annually. *Hodel v. Irving*, 481 U.S. 704, 712–13 (1987).

In an effort to redress this legacy of allotment and reform a broken system, Congress has passed a series of legislation in the last few decades attempting to consolidate lands, promote estate planning to relieve an overburden and inefficient federal probate system for Indian lands, and other systemic reforms in management of tribal lands and natural resources. Some of these attempts, with limited success, have included provisions for land to escheat to the tribal government or otherwise be consolidated with existing landowners to better manage the number of co-owners. Other legislative fixes have attempted to return some control to the tribe to administer tribal and individual Indian property. For example, in 1994, the Congress enacted the American Indian Trust Reform Act, 25 U.S.C. § 161a, § 162a, and § 4001 et seq., which created the Office of the Special Trustee (OST). The OST has primary responsibility to ensure the accountability of the Department of the Interior in managing the trust accounts for Individual Indian Monies (IIM) accounts and for tribal government trust funds.

Other efforts to address fractionation of Indian ownership include the Indian Land Consolidation Act (ILCA) of 1983, 25 U.S.C. § 2201 et seq., amendments to ILCA in 2000, and the American Indian Probate Reform Act (AIPRA) of 2004. Pursuant to AIPRA, tribal governments are encouraged to enact tribal probate codes to work in conjunction with the probate of trust lands, 25 U.S.C. § 2205.

Today, throughout Indian country, multiple co-owners share fractional property interests in single parcels of allotted lands. The lands, if held in trust by the federal government, are inalienable due to federal restrictions. The lands, if held in fee by the Indian co-tenants, become de facto inalienable because they are largely unmarketable and lack the capacity to be put to efficient economic use. Banks and other investors are cautious about lending money on lands with multiple Indian co-tenants each owning small fractional property interests, although with federal involvement and guarantees, mortgages and other security interests may be collateralized by long term leasehold interests.

D. Modern Tribal Territorial Boundaries and Indian Country

Tribal lands include all real property inside the exterior boundaries of a recognized tribal reservation or within the territorial jurisdiction of a tribe. The exterior boundaries of a Tribe's territory are generally defined by treaty language, executive order provisions, federal statute or in a property description of a land patent or deed to a large tract of land. These lands include multiple land tenure patterns and include lands owned by tribal governments, tribal businesses, American Indians and non-Indians, including lands owned by individuals and lands held in various co-ownership arrangements. The existence of non-Indian owned lands inside a tribal territory does not necessarily defeat the Indian country or tribal status of a tract of land.

1. Current Types of Property Ownership in Indian Country

a. Trust Lands

A significant percentage of Indian land holdings are held in trust and are commonly referred to as "trust lands." In this arrangement, the United States holds the legal title to property and the individual Indian(s) or Tribe holds the beneficial interest. The over 55 million acres of lands that are held in trust by the United States are subject to an overarching restraint on alienation, in that the lands cannot be sold, leased, mortgaged, or taken by eminent domain or otherwise encumbered without the consent and approval of the United States. Trust lands cannot be taxed by state or local entities but are generally treated as "federal lands" subject to substantial federal statutory and regulatory schemes.

Individual Indian trust lands are generally the outgrowth of the allotment process. Current Indian property interest holders are usually the descendants and/or the successors in interest to an original allottee that received property during the allotment process. Most individual Indian trust lands have multiple co-owners and the general administration of the land involves the United States Department of Interior as trustee, responsible for approving land transactions and accepting income derived from lands on behalf of the beneficiary. Probate and other legal matters involving trust lands come under the jurisdiction of special Department of Interior forums and, absent a federal statute to the contrary, are not heard in state or tribal probate courts.

The United States also holds lands in trust for Tribes. These lands are either lands that remained in tribal ownership following the allotment process or lands that have been put into trust for the Tribe after the 1930s. The Secretary of the Interior has the authority to take lands into trust and routinely does so under 25 U.S.C § 465 as a way of both revamping tribal land bases and as a way of reaffirming clear federal-tribal jurisdiction over a tract of land.

For instance, if a Tribe purchases a tract of fee land that it lost to the allotment process or other dispossession, the land does not become "Indian land" by the unilateral action of the Tribe becoming the fee title owner. In order to guarantee that the Tribe will have presumed jurisdiction over the land, and protect the land from state taxation and regulation and operations of state law such as eminent domain or adverse possession that could deprive the tribe of future ownership in the land, it is necessary to have the land accepted into trust status by the United States. Although there are positive consequences for the Tribes in the Secretary of the Interior's land-into-trust power, there are also downsides for the Tribes to consider. Trust status creates a restriction on alienation that protects the land, but it also takes decision-making authority away from the Tribe and places control in the federal government to make decisions regarding leasing, business development, rights-of-way and other considerations. It also means that once tribally controlled land is now "federal" land and subject to federal laws such as environmental controls and other land use regulations that the lands may not be subject to under fee ownership. Particularly in the business context, the decision of whether to place land into trust can be a difficult balance of competing concerns.

b. Restricted Lands

Federal restraints on the alienation of Indian land can also be accomplished by statute or regulation. Under this approach, legal title remains with the Tribe or individual Indian, rather than the United States, but legal restrictions keep the land from being sold or otherwise encumbered with liens or subject to state taxation. The land could later revert to fee status, either by operation of an event prescribed by statute such as the expiration of a designated time period, or by a legislative amendment lifting the restriction.

c. Fee Lands

Given the aftermath of the allotment process, where trust and restricted lands lost their protected status or large amounts of "surplus" lands were converted from tribal ownership, it is now common for both individual non-Indians and Tribes to own parcels of fee lands inside Indian country. In fact, some Tribes are the minority landowners inside their territory with the majority of lands being owned by non-tribal individuals or entities, including state and locally owned lands. Fee lands can be freely sold and are subject to state taxation. Fee lands can also be mortgaged without concern for federal or tribal consent. Probate and other administration of fee lands does not involve the federal government, even for Indian-owned lands inside Indian country.

Fee land ownership outside of Indian country is simply subject to the property law rules of jurisdiction where the property is located. If a Tribe or individual Indian purchases or acquires an interest in fee lands outside of Indian country, no special legal status attaches to that land, unless the Secretary of Interior exercises the power to take that property into trust. It is more difficult and more unlikely to see lands taken into trust unless the area where the land is located is on or near a tribal territory or original homeland.

Cherokee Nation Headquarters. Photo credit Terry G. Townsend.

2. The Future

At the time lands were allotted, it was presumed that Tribes would dissolve and, within a generation or two, there would be no tribal land base or territory. As a result, there was no long range planning or thought given to how individual Indians or the Tribes would maintain or administer land tenure systems today.

The system that followed, with federal administration of trust land, is plagued with an overall lack of local control and inefficiencies that leave much of the land base encumbered by a broken system.

In recent years, it has become clear that reform of the present system is needed from a trust management standpoint. To date, small measures have been taken to place control back at the local tribal level.

Within many Tribes there exists a tribal realty or property office that contracts with the Bureau of Indian Affairs to perform federal property functions at the tribal level, such as approving leases, transfers of property interest, land use management, the acquisition of appraisals, etc. Therefore, instead of dealing directly with the Department of Interior, individual Indians and those that seek information on the status of lands can consult local offices rather than relying on federal officials. Yet where these arrangements for tribal self-government exist, the tribal officials are carrying out a federal function pursuant to federal laws and regulations rather than implementing a land tenure system prescribed by the Tribes.

Following *Cobell v. Salazar*, 572 F.3d 808 (D.D.C. 2009), a class action lawsuit brought by Indian allottees against the United States involving claims of federal mismanagement of property and assets, the Department of Interior will reconsider reforming the current system. Past attempts at reform have not been successful in effectuating meaningful change, but have lead to minor improvements geared toward the reestablishment of tribal land bases, consolidation of ownership to address fractionated allotments, and estate planning to address a backlog in federal probate of Indian lands.

Checkpoints

- Tribal property ownership concepts continue to inform contemporary tribal property laws. Tribal realty offices implement tribal laws and regulations.

- American Indian property law is important to understanding the extent of tribal regulatory authority. Tribal reservation boundaries provide the basic area of the tribal land base. The allotment process has changed the status of land within reservation boundaries.

- The Bureau of Indian Affairs, on behalf of the U.S. government, has management authority over the more than 55 million acres of tribal land in trust status. Tribal lands in trust status are recognized under tribal regulatory authority and are exempt from state property taxation.

- The Office of Special Trustee within the Department of the Interior has the responsibility of ensuring the accountability of the U.S. government in managing trust fund accounts for American Indian owners of lands in trust status.

- The three main types of tribal property are: trust lands, restricted lands, and fee lands.

Chapter 3

Criminal Jurisdiction in Indian Country

Roadmap

- Learn that tribal societies engaged in restorative justice practices to deal with community offenders in historical times.

- Learn that contemporary tribal governments may choose to operate judicial systems with criminal jurisdiction over all Indians within the tribal territory.

- Learn that the U.S. has enacted federal laws limiting the sentencing ability of Tribal Courts for criminal offenses. In addition, federal laws allow for felony criminal jurisdiction over crimes perpetrated by American Indians or against American Indians within Indian Country.

- Understand that the federal government has enacted legislation to delegate federal criminal authority in Indian Country to state governments on a limited basis.

- Know that criminal jurisdiction analysis requires: identification of the land base upon which the crime allegedly occurred, identification of the perpetrator and the victim as American Indian or not, and cooperation between prosecuting authorities on the tribal, federal and/or state level.

- Know that Tribes retain concurrent criminal jurisdiction over any crime perpetrated by an American Indian within Indian Country.

- Know that "Indian Country" is a legal term of art defined by federal criminal statute in 18 U.S.C. § 1151.

Inherent tribal jurisdiction and sovereignty is the starting point in any analysis of jurisdiction in Indian country. The initial presumption is that a Tribe retains full jurisdiction within the tribal territory. The next step is to then determine whether any limitations have been placed upon the inherent tribal jurisdiction. In the criminal jurisdiction context, the inherent basis of tribal jurisdiction will be discussed, followed by an examination of the subsequent limitations imposed through federal statutes and judicial decisions. The two key factors of greatest significance in the analysis of criminal jurisdiction in Indian Country under Indian law are: 1) race of the alleged perpetrator and victim; and 2) ownership and status of the land where alleged criminal activity occurred. Due to the necessary analysis of these factors and other considerations in this area, criminal jurisdiction in Indian Country has been called one of the most complex areas of law. This chapter will discuss the contours of tribal criminal jurisdiction, federal criminal jurisdiction, and state criminal jurisdiction in Indian Country.

A. Tribal Criminal Jurisdiction

Tribal societies placed a high value on law and order in historical tribal communities. Often a particular clan or social group had primary responsibility for law enforcement duties in the tribal structure. Those who violated tribal laws would be dealt consequences in line with the tribal philosophy of bringing the community back into balance. These concepts of community balance between the perpetrator and society have been adapted by the restorative justice movement in the United States. Historically, tribal punishments for wrong-doers could range from public shaming, whereby the misdeeds of the community member were announced at a community gathering, to expulsion from the tribal community. Some Tribes used a permanent facial scar to mark the expelled perpetrator as unworthy of being part of a human society. In contrast and in keeping with the diversity of laws and cultural norms between various Tribes, other Tribes were known to have retributive laws that resulted in execution or severe flogging for certain offenses.

Within communities where communal balance was central, lawbreakers often faced the law enforcement clan and were informed of the actions they would be required to complete to restore the tribal communal balance. Remedial actions could include providing goods and services to a family injured by the lawbreaker's misdeeds and/or periods of solitary reflection and spiritual instruction for the lawbreaker. Behaviors detrimental to others in the community were swiftly and effectively dealt with in historical tribal communities to maintain social values and prevent further infractions stemming from the original misdeed. For repeat offenders, the consequences were steep. Banishment from the tribal community, family and friends was viewed as one of the most severe punishments handed down to an offender. The tribal way of life ensured a sense of belonging, protection, and social goodwill, without which the human existence would be desolate and solitary. Another extreme punishment employed by some tribal communities for a recurring offender would be death.

1. Contemporary Tribal Justice Systems, Tribal Constitutional Rights, and Criminal Sentencing

In contemporary times, there are approximately 200 federally-recognized tribal justice systems currently in operation in the United States. Tribal justice systems may have all or some of the following components: tribal court system, tribal public defender services, tribal probation office, tribal law enforcement department, and tribal detention center. Tribal governments are in the first instance responsible for funding tribal justice systems. The Bureau of Indian Affairs has oversight for federal funding of tribal justice systems. Within the U.S. Department of Justice, federal funding opportunities are offered through the Office of Tribal Justice for high priority tribal safety needs on a grant basis for establishing or upgrading tribal justice systems.

The Indian Self-Determination and Education Assistance Act of 1975, Public Law 93-638, provided a process whereby tribal governments may enter into a contract with the BIA for services provided in tribal communities. Most of the law enforcement departments operated by Tribes are administered under this type of contract from the BIA for federal funding. Components not maintained by a Tribe are the responsibility of the BIA for law and order in Indian Country. The BIA provides training for both BIA and tribal police officers at the Indian Police Academy in Artesia, New Mexico. One of the common constraints of tribal law enforcement is the underfunding of these departments to the detriment of tribal communities. The National Congress of American Indians (NCAI) has estimated that the number of active duty BIA and tribal law enforcement officers is currently at half the amount needed to adequately meet public safety needs in Indian Country. In the regular course of work for tribal law enforcement, alleged perpetrators in Indian Country are arrested and subject to prosecution as defendants in tribal courts.

Defendants within the criminal jurisdiction of a Tribe may rely on tribal laws, and where applicable the tribal constitution, to uphold their rights to due process under such laws. The Indian Civil Rights Act passed in 1968 provided guidelines to tribal justice systems on adopting a modified version of the U.S. Bill of Rights, 25 U.S.C. § 1302(a). An early U.S. Supreme Court decision, *Talton v. Mayes*, 163 U.S. 376 (1896), had previously held that the U.S. Bill of Rights was not applicable to tribal governments as separate sovereigns. In the *Santa Clara Pueblo v. Martinez*, 436 U.S. 49 (1978), case, the U.S. Supreme Court interpreted the Indian Civil Rights Act as providing only habeas corpus relief for those challenging detainment by a tribal jurisdiction and not providing any further cause of action in federal court against a tribal government. 436 U.S. at 69. Therefore, those alleging wrongful detention by a tribal justice system may seek relief under the ICRA, 25 U.S.C. § 1303, and file a habeas corpus petition in federal court seeking release. Other due process rights asserted in a tribal court proceeding must be based upon tribal laws or provisions in the tribal constitution and remedied within the tribal court system, not the federal courts. The importance of adopting some key constitutional rights outlined in the ICRA is reflected in the increased sentencing ability of tribal courts when providing procedural safeguards outlined in the 2010 Tribal Law and Order Act.

Tribal courts exercising criminal jurisdiction employ, either through a permanent position or through a contract for services, a tribal prosecutor. Increasingly, tribal court systems include a tribally-funded public defender position as well for those criminally charged in the court system. Recent developments in federal Indian law under the Tribal Law and Order Act (TLOA) of 2010 provide an incentive for offering public defender services by permitting those court systems greater sentencing capabilities than those that do not offer such services. Under the Indian Civil Rights Act (ICRA), 25 U.S.C. § 1301 et seq., tribal courts may sentence an Indian offender up to one year of incarceration and/or a fine of $5,000 for any one offense, 25 U.S.C. § 1302(a)(7)(B). Tribal courts meeting the additional due process safeguards requirements enacted through the TLOA may sentence an Indian offender up to three years of incarceration and/or a fine of up to $15,000 for an offense under tribal law, 25 U.S.C. § 1302(a)(7)(C).

For the greater sentencing authority, the tribal judge may impose the increased sentence where the defendant has a prior conviction in any U.S. jurisdiction for the same or a similar offense or where the defendant is charged with an offense that would be subject to more than one year incarceration in a federal or state criminal proceeding, 25 U.S.C. § 1302(b)(1), (2). When sentencing beyond the basic one year incarceration and/or $5,000 fine, there are five basic rights that must be provided to the defendant. 25 U.S.C. § 1302(c) provides the following requirements for tribal judges to exercise the three year and/or $15,000 fine per offense greater sentencing authority.

(c) Rights of defendants
In a criminal proceeding in which an Indian tribe, in exercising powers of self-government, imposes a total term of imprisonment of more than 1 year on a defendant, the Indian tribe shall—
(1) provide to the defendant the right to effective assistance of counsel at least equal to that guaranteed by the United States Constitution; and
(2) at the expense of the tribal government, provide an indigent defendant the assistance of a defense attorney licensed to practice law by any jurisdiction in the United States that applies appropriate pro-

fessional licensing standards and effectively ensures the competence and professional responsibility of its licensed attorneys;

(3) require that the judge presiding over the criminal proceeding—

(A) has sufficient legal training to preside over criminal proceedings; and

(B) is licensed to practice law by any jurisdiction in the United States;

(4) prior to charging the defendant, make publicly available the criminal laws (including regulations and interpretative documents), rules of evidence, and rules of criminal procedure (including rules governing the recusal of judges in appropriate circumstances) of the tribal government; and

(5) maintain a record of the criminal proceeding, including an audio or other recording of the trial proceeding.

When a tribal court meets all of these requirements, then the imposition of greater sentences will allow the court to better match punishment with the severity of an offense committed by a defendant subject to tribal prosecution. There are added financial costs for a tribal judicial system to meet the increased procedural safeguards.

Federal criminal courts in Indian Country also exist for those Tribes without an established court system. These federal courts, Courts of Indian Offenses, are commonly referred to as "CFR courts" because the operative criminal law is contained in the Code of Federal Regulations for Indian Country crimes. 25 CFR 11.100 provides a listing of the Tribes served by such courts at present. A majority of the CFR courts remain in what was formerly known as "Indian Territory," within the current state of Oklahoma and are serving Tribal Nations in that region. Information is available online about specific tribal courts through the Tribal Court Clearinghouse website.

2. Tribal Criminal Jurisdiction Contracting and Expanding in Recent Decades

The Indian Civil Rights Act of 1968, 25 U.S.C. §§ 1301 and 1302, provides the basic limitations imposed by the federal government on the exercise of tribal criminal jurisdiction. While tribal criminal codes provide the punishable offenses in tribal courts accompanied by sentencing guidelines, the ICRA has limitations on the extent of criminal jurisdiction over defendants and the sentencing ability of tribal courts. Since the decision in *Oliphant v. Suquamish,* 435 U.S. 191 (1978), the U.S. Supreme Court has imposed limitations on tribal criminal jurisdiction over non-Indians through the concept known as "implicit divestiture." This divestiture is purportedly a result of the categorization of tribal governments as "domestic dependent nations." The U.S. Supreme Court stated in the *Oliphant* decision that through the incorporation of tribal governments into the United States certain aspects of tribal sovereignty have been lost, including criminal jurisdiction over non-Indians within tribal territories. In some instances, the U.S. Congress has responded to provide recognition for the inherent sovereign authority of tribal governments and judicial systems where the U.S. Supreme Court has found a limitation.

In the U.S. Supreme Court case, *Oliphant v. Suquamish Tribe,* 435 U.S. 191 (1978), the Court held that tribal governments and judicial systems lacked criminal jurisdiction over any non-Indian in the tribal territory regardless of the alleged offense. Subsequently in *Duro v. Reina,* 495 U.S. 676 (1990), the U.S. Supreme Court held that Tribes have criminal jurisdiction only over their own tribal members and not over other Indians. Both of these U.S. Supreme Court holdings limiting tribal criminal jurisdiction have been modified by later federal law.

Closely following the *Duro* decision, tribal leadership joined together nationally to seek federal legislation remedying the jurisdictional gap that was created through the Court's decision—namely, the complexity that would follow requiring law enforcement to first identify specific tribal enrollment for alleged Indian perpetrators before handling criminal situations. The U.S. Congress swiftly passed an amendment to the ICRA on November 5, 1990 acknowledging tribal criminal jurisdiction over all Indians in the tribal territory. The definitional section of the ICRA was amended at 25 U.S.C. § 1301(2) to read: "'powers of self-government' means and includes all governmental powers possessed by an Indian tribe, executive, legislative, and judicial, and all offices, bodies, and tribunals by and through which they are executed, including courts of Indian offenses; and means the inherent power of Indian tribes, hereby recognized and affirmed, to exercise criminal jurisdiction over *all Indians* (emphasis added)." This amendment is commonly referred to as the "*Duro* fix" which effectively negated the U.S. Supreme Court's limitation on tribal criminal jurisdiction in the *Duro v. Reina* decision. Today, tribal court systems handle prosecutions of tribal members and all other Indians committing crimes within the tribal territory they oversee.

In the mid 2000s, reports of widespread violence against Native American women in tribal territories due to non-Indian perpetrators were widely publicized. With the jurisdictional gap created by the *Oliphant* decision leaving prosecution of non-Indians committing crimes in Indian Country to either federal or state law enforcement, the victimization of Native American women reached epidemic proportions when those external law enforcement entities were not diligent in bringing prosecutions. This jurisdictional gap was particularly apparent when sexual violence is perpetrated by a non-Indian male against an Indian female on tribal lands. The seriousness of such widespread sexual violence was reported on by Amnesty International USA in 2007 through a report titled, *"Maze of Injustice: The Failure to Protect Indigenous Women from Sexual Violence in the USA."* In the introductory chapter of the report, an overview of the violence experienced by American Indian women reveals staggering statistics.

> Over the past decade, federal government studies have consistently shown that American Indian and Alaska Native women experience much higher levels of sexual violence than other women in the USA. Data gathered by the US Department of Justice indicates that Native American and Alaska Native women are more than 2.5 times more likely to be raped or sexually assaulted than women in the USA in general. A US Department of Justice study on violence against women concluded that 34.1 percent of American Indian and Alaska Native women — or more than one in three — will be raped during their lifetime; the comparable figure for the USA as a whole is less than one in five. Shocking though these statistics are, it is widely believed that they do not accurately portray the extent of sexual violence against Native American and Alaska Native women. Additionally, the 2010 Tribal Law and Order Act (TLOA) included direction to the U.S. (*Maze of Injustice*, pg. 2).

Also noted in the report is the maze that an Indian woman must navigate in bringing a non-Indian perpetrator to justice for rape and/or acts of sexual violence. Response times are impacted when tribal, state, and federal law enforcement need to determine the proper jurisdiction. Further, due to the known barriers to bring charges against alleged perpetrators, a substantial number of these types of crimes go unreported.

One of the attempted solutions tribal governments have employed for this law enforcement problem is to enter into cross-deputization agreements with local county and state law enforcement agencies to allow tribal and state officers response authority when criminal activity occurs in Indian Country regardless of the racial status of the perpetrator. Another potential avenue is for tribal law enforcement to work closely with the U.S. Department of Justice and U.S. attorneys for interagency coordination to respond to non-Indian crime on tribal lands. Without full criminal jurisdiction over all those who enter the tribal territory, tribal governments and communities must rely on external agencies to curb lawlessness and violence stemming from non-Indian activity within the tribal jurisdiction.

In the 2010 Tribal Law and Order Act (TLOA), the law included direction to the U.S. attorneys serving Indian Country to provide information on when federal prosecutions are declined; the appointment of a Tribal Liaison in each district office serving Indian Country; and coordination with tribal law enforcement on criminal investigations and prosecutions in tribal courts. The TLOA required an assessment by federal and tribal officials on the needs for tribal detention facilities in Indian Country, including juvenile detention facilities and construction of federal detention centers. The U.S. Department of Justice maintains a web site on "Tribal Justice and Safety" which provides information on implementation of the TLOA, current grant opportunities for Tribes to participate in law enforcement training, and reports from tribal consultations and advisory groups, http://www.justice.gov/tribal/index.html. When an alleged perpetrator is an American Indian on tribal lands, felony criminal acts of sexual violence would be within both tribal and federal criminal jurisdiction.

3. Partial Federal Response to Non-Indian Perpetrators in Indian Country: The Tribal Exercise of Special Domestic Violence Jurisdiction under Federal Law

In March of 2013, the Violence Against Women Act (VAWA) was reauthorized and included amendments to the Indian Civil Rights Act recognizing the inherent authority of tribal governments and judicial systems "to exercise special domestic violence jurisdiction *over all persons* (emphasis added)." This provision is set to go into effect starting two years after the date of enactment when a tribal government requests inclusion as a participating Tribe. For those Tribes seeking quicker implementation, they may apply for pilot project status with the U.S. Attorney General and provide verification that all procedural safeguards required have been met. Thus, the holding in *Oliphant* has been partially modified by federal law recognizing that when the offense alleged is domestic violence, dating violence or violation of a protection order, then federally-approved tribal courts may prosecute non-Indians committing such an offense against an Indian person within the tribal territory.

As with the greater sentencing available under the Tribal Law and Order Act of 2010, the special domestic violence jurisdiction has additional requirements for tribal courts to carry out the new federal law. First, the special jurisdiction applies to certain persons on tribal lands. It will not apply when a non-Indian perpetrator commits domestic violence against a non-Indian victim within the tribal territory. The non-Indian perpetrator must have a tie to the participating Tribe seeking prosecution, such as residing in the Tribe's Indian Country; being employed by the Tribe; or being in an intimate relationship with an Indian resident or tribal member. Second, the alleged non-Indian perpetrator will be subject to the special tribal criminal jurisdiction if the alleged criminal conduct occurs in the Tribe's Indian Country and falls into any of the following categories: domestic violence, dating violence, or violations of protection orders.

Next, the tribal court must employ certain procedural safeguards to exercise the special domestic violence jurisdiction over non-Indians. Two particular safeguards include the right to an impartial jury and the right to file a federal habeas corpus petition to federal court challenging the tribal court's jurisdiction and an additional petition to stay detention by the Tribe. The impartial jury requirements include drawing from a cross section of the community and not systematically excluding non-Indians or other distinctive community groups from serving on the tribal court jury.

With this special domestic violence jurisdiction, tribal courts will be in a better position to address the violence suffered by Indian women caused by non-Indian dating, spousal or intimate partners on tribal lands. Underscoring this exercise of tribal criminal jurisdiction is the explicit continuing concurrent authority of federal and state law enforcement and judicial systems. The extent of federal and state criminal jurisdiction will be more fully discussed in the next sections.

B. Federal Criminal Jurisdiction: Federal Court Decisions and Federal Legislation Impacting Tribal Criminal Jurisdiction

A major impetus for the development of federal Indian law has arisen from the area of criminal law. Prior to the removal and reservation eras, the United States entered into treaties with Tribal Nations often with terms requiring each side to punish offenders harming the other side. Some treaties required a Tribe to turn over captive U.S. citizens and others recognized tribal authority to punish trespassing U.S. citizens in tribal territories. As the removal and reservation eras were underway, the federal officials in the BIA sought greater control over criminal matters in Indian Country.

The next section will provide the relevant federal statutory and federal judicial opinion underpinnings for four types of criminal jurisdiction in Indian Country: 1) federal criminal jurisdiction over Indian perpetrators; 2) federal prosecution of crimes between Indians and non-Indians; 3) criminal jurisdiction over non-Indian perpetrators; and 4) state criminal jurisdiction over Indian perpetrators. The following laws apply only when the alleged crime occurred in Indian Country as defined in 18 U.S.C. § 1151.

1. Extension of Federal Criminal Jurisdiction into Indian Country over Indian Perpetrators

The primary historical case demonstrating the tension between federal officials seeking criminal prosecution of tribal citizens and tribal sovereignty was *Ex Parte Crow Dog,* 109 U.S. 556 (1883). The lawsuit reached the U.S. Supreme Court as a habeas corpus petition for wrongful imprisonment by the U.S. of Crow Dog in the Dakota Territory for the crime of murder of another Indian leader, Spotted Tail. Crow Dog had been tried and sentenced to execution in federal court. The U.S. Supreme Court held that the U.S. lacked jurisdiction over Crow Dog for his actions in his tribal territory against another tribal person, rejecting arguments that treaties or federal statutes extended federal authority into tribal jurisdictions for tribal citizen prosecution. The BIA seized upon the case to build political pressure to extend federal criminal jurisdiction into Indian Country. The efforts led to the passage of the Major Crimes Act (MCA) of 1885, 18 U.S.C. § 1153, listing the felony level crimes permitting an alleged Indian perpetrator to be charged and tried in federal court. The listed crimes have been updated and modified since 1885. A recent modification included expanding the specific felony assault crimes listed to match the general broader catalog of federal assault crimes contained in 18 U.S.C. § 113 as under the MCA federal jurisdiction if committed in Indian Country.

The Major Crimes Act represented a significant departure from the limited authority of the U.S. Congress in the U.S. Constitution to regulate commerce with Indian Tribes. The constitutional authority for the MCA was swiftly challenged in *U.S. v. Kagama,* 118 U.S. 375 (1886). The U.S. Supreme Court addressed the central issue as a question of federal or state criminal jurisdiction over the alleged Indian perpetrator on the Hoopa Valley Reservation. The Court reasoned that the federal government should act as a shield for the defendant from state prosecution.

> These Indian tribes *are* wards of the nation. They are communities dependent on the United States.... Because of the local ill feeling, the people of the States where they are found are often their deadliest enemies. From their very weakness and helplessness, so largely due to the course of dealing of the Federal Government with them and the treaties

in which it has been promised, there arises a duty of protection, and with it the power. This has always been recognized by the Executive and by Congress, and by this court, whenever the question has arisen. 118 U.S. at 383–384.

Thus, the constitutionality of the MCA was upheld as within a protective power of the U.S. Congress over Indian affairs in this decision. The Court relied on a policy rationale rather than finding support in the text of the U.S. Constitution to uphold this extension of federal jurisdiction into tribal community affairs.

To apply the Major Crimes Act for federal prosecution, it must be included in the indictment and proven beyond a reasonable doubt that the defendant is an Indian, the crime occurred in Indian Country, and the victim was an Indian. Different tests have arisen in the Eighth Circuit courts and the Ninth Circuit courts to determine whether a person qualifies as "Indian" under the MCA.

The Eighth Circuit Court of Appeals in *U.S. v. Stymiest*, 581 F.3d 759 (8th Cir. 2009) announced five factors to be considered equally for a jury determination on whether the defendant qualified as an Indian person: 1) enrollment in a Tribe, 2) government recognition formally or informally through providing the defendant assistance reserved only to Indians, 3) tribal recognition formally or informally through subjecting the defendant to tribal court jurisdiction, 4) enjoying benefits of tribal affiliation, and 5) social recognition as an Indian through living on a reservation and participating in Indian social life, including whether the defendant holds himself out as an Indian. (581 F.3d at 763). The Ninth Circuit Court of Appeals test is composed of two parts: 1) defendant must have some Indian blood; and 2) defendant must be "recognized" as an Indian by a Tribe or by the federal government. See *U.S. v. Cruz*, 554 F.3d 840 (9th Cir. 2009). Therefore, the Eighth Circuit test is much broader, allowing the inclusion of a person for federal criminal prosecution as an Indian when the same person may not be eligible as an Indian for tribal citizenship or federal services. Since the passage of the MCA, Congress has passed several other notable statutes regarding criminal jurisdiction in Indian Country.

2. Federal Prosecution for Crime between Indians and Non-Indians in Indian Country

For crimes not specifically listed in the MCA, federal criminal jurisdiction extends over Indians that commit crimes in Indian Country against non-Indians under the Indian Country Crimes Act (ICCA), 18 U.S.C. § 1152, commonly referred to as the "General Crimes Act." The ICCA also applies when a non-Indian perpetrator commits a crime against an Indian in Indian Country. This federal law does not apply if any of the following exceptions are met: 1) as mentioned, the crime(s) was by an Indian against an Indian or the property of an Indian; 2) crimes by an Indian where the tribal jurisdiction has provided punishment under local tribal law; or 3) to offenses under the exclusive jurisdiction of the Tribe by treaty.

The U.S. Supreme Court held in *Williams v. U.S*, 327 U.S. 711 (1946) that the Assimilative Crimes Act, 18 U.S.C. § 13, is operative in Indian Country to allow federal prosecutions based on state criminal law where federal criminal law over an offense is lacking. This federal statute provides further federal criminal jurisdiction over Indian perpetrators committing acts against non-Indians in Indian Country. By applying the Assimilative Crimes Act, federal prosecutions of Indian perpetrators extend to crimes listed under a state criminal code. When the federal criminal code does not have a particular crime listed and the state criminal code does include the offense, Indian perpetrators can be federally prosecuted using the Assimilative Crimes Act to bring the offense to federal court.

3. Criminal Jurisdiction over Non-Indian Perpetrators in Indian Country

As discussed previously, tribal criminal jurisdiction over non-Indians has been sharply curtailed by the U.S. Supreme Court's decision in *Oliphant v. Suquamish Tribe*, 435 U.S. 191 (1978). In the *Oliphant* decision, the Court opined that tribal governments lacked inherent criminal jurisdiction over non-Indians as a general matter since the formation of the United States and the extension of U.S. boundaries surrounding the Tribes. Further, the Court found significant that Congress had not enacted a federal law recognizing tribal criminal jurisdiction over non-Indians and thus, held that Tribes could not exercise such jurisdiction absent an act of Congress. Due to this U.S. Supreme Court opinion, tribal courts do not generally exercise criminal jurisdiction over non-Indian perpetrators committing crimes within the tribal territory. Indian law scholars have criticized this judicial result and the subsequent lack of law enforcement supervision over non-Indians occurring in many parts of Indian Country.

With the 2013 passage of amendments to the Indian Civil Rights Act, tribal courts may exercise special domestic violence jurisdiction over non-Indians when meeting certain federal requirements. This special tribal jurisdiction partially modified the *Oliphant* decision and recognized the inherent authority of tribal criminal jurisdiction over all persons committing acts of domestic violence against Indians in the tribal territory. This special tribal jurisdiction exists concurrently with federal criminal jurisdiction and/or state jurisdiction where appropriate.

If a non-Indian commits a crime against an Indian in Indian Country, then under the ICCA federal criminal jurisdiction applies. If the crime is not a federal crime, but would be considered a state crime, then the Assimilative Crimes Act allows federal prosecution of the criminal act(s) with state criminal law underlying the prosecution. If no federal prosecution is brought against the non-Indian perpetrator, then the tribal authorities are without criminal jurisdiction to prevent further criminal acts by the non-Indian or to punish the non-Indian due to the *Oliphant* decision, unless the criminal conduct falls within the categories of domestic violence, dating violence or violation of a protection order. The 2010 TLOA included a provision requiring U.S. attorneys to compile data on criminal cases arising in Indian Country that are declined for federal prosecution to provide information on what types of cases are not being prosecuted, the extent of declinations and to assess the effectiveness of federal criminal officers in tribal territories.

If a non-Indian commits a crime against a non-Indian in Indian Country, then the U.S. Supreme Court has held that federal criminal jurisdiction does not apply. In *U.S. v. McBratney,* 104 U.S. 621 (1882), the Court held that exclusive state criminal jurisdiction existed where only non-Indians are perpetrator and victim in criminal acts occurring within Indian Country. Therefore, the state law enforcement must act upon these types of crimes within Indian Country and prosecute the non-Indian perpetrators in state courts.

4. State Criminal Jurisdiction over Indian Perpetrators in Indian Country

During the termination era of U.S. Indian policy, Congress passed legislation in 1953 delegating federal criminal jurisdiction over Indians and non-Indians in Indian Country to certain state governments through passage of Public Law 280, commonly referred to as "PL-280," 18 U.S.C. § 1162(a). Six states assumed mandatory criminal jurisdiction under PL-280: Alaska, California, Minnesota, Nebraska, Oregon, and Wisconsin. Exceptions to the reach of PL-280 exist for the mandatory states. For example, the Metlakatla Indian Community has concurrent criminal jurisdiction with the state in Alaska. In Minnesota, the Red Lake Band of Chippewa is excepted from state criminal jurisdiction. The Warm Springs Reservation is not within Oregon's PL-280 jurisdiction. Wisconsin does not have state criminal jurisdiction over the Menominee Tribe.

In the mandatory PL-280 states, the Major Crimes Act and Indian Country Crimes Act were no longer operative, 18 U.S.C. § 1162(c). Thus, there is state criminal law and state criminal prosecution for all crimes committed in Indian Country by Indians and non-Indians in the mandatory states. PL-280 has worked as a delegation of federal authority to state governments for criminal jurisdiction in Indian Country. PL-280 also contained a civil component providing access to state courts in matters involving Indians in Indian Country, 28 U.S.C. § 1360.

Up through 1968, other state governments could optionally accept the delegation of federal criminal jurisdiction and tailor the delegation to certain types of criminal activity. For example, Idaho optionally accepted PL-280 authority under state legislation for seven specific areas: 1) compulsory school attendance; 2) juvenile delinquency and youth rehabilitation; 3) dependent, neglected and abused children; 4) insanities and mental illness; 5) public assistance; 6) domestic relations; and 7) operation and management of motor vehicles upon highways and roads maintained by the county or state, or political subdivisions. Idaho Code § 67-5101. All other areas of criminal jurisdiction enforced federally remain available for federal prosecution either under the Major Crimes Act or the Indian Country Crimes Act.

The option for states to immediately receive federal criminal jurisdiction in Indian Country existed up until the passage of the Indian Civil Rights Act of 1968 which included a provision that tribal consent was necessary prior to assumption of federal criminal jurisdiction by states, 25 U.S.C. § 1321(a). PL-280 has been critically regarded based upon lack of federal funding to those states assuming jurisdiction and lack of state law enforcement with jurisdiction adequately policing Indian Country. State retrocession of criminal jurisdiction is available under 25 U.S.C. § 1323 by sending a state resolution to the Secretary of the Interior for consideration of a request to relinquish the delegation of federal criminal jurisdiction in Indian Country. With passage of the Tribal Law and Order Act (TLOA) in 2010, tribal governments now have the authority to request a return of federal criminal jurisdiction where PL-280 jurisdiction has been exercised by the state, 18 U.S.C. § 1162(d). States may also pass legislation for a process for retrocession of PL-280 jurisdiction initiated by a tribal government request, which the state of Washington did in March 2012.

State criminal jurisdiction in Indian Country may also exist based upon state-specific legislation passed by Congress. Under 25 U.S.C. § 232, New York in 1948 assumed all criminal jurisdiction in Indian Country within state borders. Similarly, Kansas in 1948 obtained specific legislation for state criminal jurisdiction in Indian Country, 18 U.S.C. § 3243. North Dakota also has a federal grant of criminal jurisdiction over Indian Country under 60 stat. 229 passed in 1946. Congress may also pass specific criminal jurisdiction laws on a tribe-specific basis or in Indian land claim settlement acts. For example, the

Mashantucket Pequot Tribe through the Connecticut Indian Land Claims Settlement Act in 1983 is under state criminal jurisdiction, 25 U.S.C. § 1755.

C. Concurrent Prosecutions of Indian Perpetrators in Federal, State, and Tribal Courts

Tribal courts have inherent criminal jurisdiction over Indian perpetrators committing crimes in the tribal territory. With the extension of federal criminal jurisdiction, and at times state criminal jurisdiction, in Indian Country, the question has arisen whether tribal court prosecution of the Indian perpetrator for a crime bars a second prosecution in federal or state court. The Fifth Amendment of the U.S. Constitution prohibits double prosecution, known as "double jeopardy," of the same individual by the same sovereign jurisdiction. In *U.S. v. Wheeler,* 435 U.S. 313 (1978), the U.S. Supreme Court held that a tribal criminal prosecution of a tribal citizen was the action of a separate sovereign and therefore, the federal prosecution of the same individual for the same crime was not in violation of the double jeopardy clause. After the Indian Civil Rights Act was amended to recognize tribal inherent jurisdiction over all Indians within a Tribe's territory, a case was brought into the U.S. Supreme Court challenging that provision and the prosecution of a non-member Indian by both a tribal court and a federal court.

In *U.S. v. Lara,* 541 U.S. 193 (2004), the U.S. Supreme Court upheld the authority of Congress to recognize inherent tribal criminal jurisdiction over non-member Indians, in essence upholding the "*Duro* fix." Further, the Court determined that no double jeopardy violation occurred when the non-member Indian was prosecuted in a tribal court and subsequently in federal court for the same criminal actions. It reasoned that each court was maintained by a separate sovereign and therefore, no double jeopardy had occurred for the Indian defendant in the two separate criminal prosecutions. This reasoning holds true for Indian defendants prosecuted in a tribal court system and subsequently in a state court system with proper criminal jurisdiction. It should be noted that few defendants in the tribal justice systems seek to challenge the authority of tribal prosecutions.

In conclusion, tribal courts continue to have concurrent criminal jurisdiction under tribal laws to prosecute Indians where there is federal criminal jurisdiction or where state criminal jurisdiction exists by virtue of PL-280 or a specific federal law. Because of inherent tribal criminal jurisdiction over Indians, a Tribe does not relinquish its authority over criminal matters in the tribal territory by not exercising that authority. It is within the tribal prosecutorial authority to charge all offenses committed in the tribal territory to the limits of tribal sentencing maximums. One of the major federal limitations on the tribal prosecutorial authority is derived from the *Oliphant* decision barring prosecutions of non-Indians by tribal courts. Secondly, federal law has placed maximum sentencing limitations on tribal courts per offense for Indian defendants under the ICRA of one year incarceration and/or up to a $5,000 fine with those maximums increasing up to three years of incarceration and/or up to a $15,000 fine when procedural safeguards are met under federal law.

Overall, tribal courts are effectively dealing with the daily prosecutions of Indian offenders in Indian Country. Tribal law enforcement has the task of handing over Indian perpetrators to the tribal justice system and referring non-Indian perpetrators to state and federal authorities. The jurisdictional gap is found when there is not a proper response from state and federal authorities with jurisdiction over offenders committing crimes in Indian Country.

Checkpoints

- Criminal jurisdiction in Indian Country requires an analysis of the land status where the crime allegedly occurred. Next, the determination of whether the perpetrator and/or victim was or was not an American Indian will establish what authorities have criminal jurisdiction.

- The U.S. Supreme Court has held that a non-Indian perpetrator committing a crime against a non-Indian victim in Indian Country is subject to state criminal jurisdiction.

- Tribes have concurrent jurisdiction with any other prosecuting authority for crimes involving American Indian perpetrators. Criminal sentencing in Tribal Courts is limited by the Indian Civil Rights Act.

- The U.S. Supreme Court has held that Tribes lack criminal jurisdiction over non-Indian perpetrators committing crimes against Indians in Indian Country. Federal legislation has allowed for limited tribal criminal jurisdiction upon approval by the Department of Justice over non-Indian perpetrators of domestic violence against Indians in Indian Country.

- Under Public Law 280, certain states have been delegated criminal jurisdiction over American Indians in Indian Country. Each reservation requires an analysis of this delegated jurisdiction in those states. Tribal criminal jurisdiction is concurrent with those state governments.

- Prosecution of an American Indian by a tribal authority and a federal or state authority for the same crime does not constitute double jeopardy under the U.S. Constitution.

Chapter 4

Tribal Government, Civil Jurisdiction and Regulation

Roadmap

- Learn that tribal governments are fully operational on tribal lands, providing basic governmental services to all those who live in tribal communities.

- Learn that tribal governance has been greatly impacted by shifting U.S. Indian policies and the current U.S. Indian policy is Indian self-determination.

- Understand that many tribal governments currently operate under tribal constitutions modeled after the U.S. system as a result of the Indian Reorganization Act of 1934.

- Understand that U.S. Supreme Court decisions have limited tribal regulatory authority in some instances over non-Indian activity on fee lands within tribal territorial boundaries.

- Know that tribal governments have various levels of administrative agencies and engage in legislative and rule-making processes similar to other governments.

This chapter will provide a broad view of contemporary tribal government and the operation of civil adjudicative and regulatory jurisdiction in Indian Country. The civil side of society is the day-to-day operation of government and law. Tribal governments are responsible for the community's facility infrastructure, basic services to tribal citizenry and those within the tribal territory, and for carrying out the governmental tasks for the society to function.

In the legal field, the law is divided into the criminal and the civil sectors. Criminal jurisdiction involves the punishment and deterrence of behavior by the society as a whole through government action carried out by the tribal prosecutor and tribal court system. Civil jurisdiction involves the private and governmental sectors operating in all other areas of law. Civil jurisdiction includes a wide variety of governmental action, commercial activity, the enforcement of rights and benefits, and all other legal interactions that are non-criminal. In civil cases, the end result can be one of the following: money damages, an injunction to stop an action sued upon, a declaratory order setting forth the rights of the parties, or requiring an action to fulfill promises previously made between parties. The civil jurisdiction stemming from tribal sovereignty will be discussed in this chapter.

A. Tribal Governments and Shifting U.S. Policies

To understand the current structure and function of tribal governments, two important elements provide context. First, Tribal Nations have had a system of governance from time immemorial and second, the U.S., since the late 1800s, has heavily impacted the contemporary organization of tribal government. As governments, Tribes are sovereign by consent of the tribal citizenry. In the discussion to follow, the sovereignty of Tribal Nations has been redefined in U.S federal Indian law through various policy eras and political movements. Tribal governance has been adaptive through contact with Euro-American politics and ideology. The negotiated relationship between Tribal Nations and the U.S. is ever-changing and evolving on issues of jurisdiction and sovereign authority.

1. Overview of Historical Tribal Governments

Historically, tribal governments were among the earliest democracies in the world. The authority of a government, known as sovereignty, was fully enjoyed by tribal governments prior to engaging in trade with European representatives. Tribal governments were generally organized with distinct internal societies responsible for governance over a specific aspect of tribal life. Family groupings occurred within clan systems that organized domestic events and coordinated social roles. Societies, on the other hand, operated as closed associations that required an invitation to join based upon a citizen's qualifications for the particular society. For example, men's societies included warrior societies, spiritual leader societies, and others focused on male activities. Women's societies included community leader societies, spiritual leader societies, and others focused on female activities. Authority passed from society to society based on the seasonal needs and events of the community in peace times. In war times, authority was grounded in the societies dealing with crisis activities, such as moving the community or harvesting crops for transport.

Tribal governments also entered into larger alliances and confederacies based upon kinship and regional cooperation. Along the eastern seaboard, the Iroquois Confederacy is an example of six separate Tribal Nations joining together

Jicarilla Apache Veteran in Summer Parade. Photo credit Angelique EagleWoman.

for regional strength, commercial benefits and diplomatic relations. From the writings of Benjamin Franklin, the Iroquois Confederacy was the main template for the uniting of the British colonies to form the United States government. In many regions of North America, tribal governments joined with each other to form stronger, larger communities and commercial networks. This practice has continued in contemporary times with the formation of organizations, such as the National Congress of American Indians providing the means for unifying tribal leadership on national issues of common concern.

2. The Impact of U.S. Indian Policy Eras on Tribal Governments

With the formation of the United States, tribal governments dealt with two opposing policies of the new government. One was respect for Tribal Nations due to their size and political strength and the other was an intention to overtake the lands and resources of Tribal Nations for the benefit of the U.S. During the sovereign-to-sovereign era of U.S. Indian policy, many treaties were negotiated between U.S. officials and Tribal Nation leaders across the country. However, in some instances, U.S. representatives purposefully bypassed legitimate tribal leadership to negotiate uneven bargains with unauthorized tribal citizens for large land cessions. As the pendulum swing began in U.S. Indian policy between the two divergent goals of recognizing tribal sovereignty and denying tribal sovereignty, the next three eras demonstrated the shifting relations between Tribal Nations and the U.S.

The removal and reservation eras of U.S. Indian policy overlap and reflect the divergence in policy-making by U.S. officials. In contravention of treaty boundaries, the U.S. through the passage of the 1830 Indian Removal Act shifted into a federal push to remove all tribal citizens on the eastern seaboard to a territory west of the Mississippi River. Contemporaneously and subsequently, U.S. officials were entering into new treaties recognizing tribal territorial boundaries and land cessions in the interior and western regions of mid-North America. Therefore, the recognition of tribal reserved lands as reservation homelands overlapped with the history for other Tribes of removal from their ancestral lands.

For most Tribes, a complete disruption in tribal governmental authority occurred during the allotment/assimilation era of the late 1800s and early 1900s. This era was marked by detrimental U.S. laws and actions intended to exert complete social control over tribal citizens. Tribal leadership was undermined by U.S.-appointed Indian agents with totalitarian control on most reservations and usually with a nearby military fort to implement agent action. During this time period, the majority of treaty-recognized reserved homelands became subject to the General Allotment Act of 1887. Through this U.S. law, tribally-owned lands were divided into small allotments distributed to individuals with little reserved to the tribal government. External pressure from U.S. officials, agents and policy-makers devastated tribal economies, governance, territorial stewardship and, through the mandatory boarding school policy for tribal children, the fabric of the tribal family. Underground tribal leader meetings allowed for a sense of tribal continuity for those able to escape the attention of the Indian agent. During this era, the Courts of Indian Offenses came into existence and imposed criminal punishments for engaging in tribal ceremonial or social activities outlawed by the agents of the BIA. By 1928, a government-commissioned task force headed by Lewis Meriam released a report, commonly known as the Meriam Report, detailing the deplorable living conditions for most tribal citizens under the authority of the BIA.

To address the deteriorating situation on reservations, federal legislation was passed in 1934 partially reaffirming recognition for tribal governmental authority, the Indian Reorganization Act (IRA), 25 U.S.C. § 461 et seq. Critically analyzing the IRA, one of the strongest components of the federal law was to authorize the BIA to provide template constitutions for adoption by tribal citizens restructuring tribal governance into a centralized tribal council. A primary benefit of restructuring under the IRA was the partial relinquishment of Indian agent control over tribal resources, laws, and citizenry. As discussed in Chapter 2 American Indian Property Law, the IRA also halted the allotment of Indian lands and allowed for the reacquisition of land into tribal ownership.

With tribal government organized under constitutions, tribal leaders began the long process of rebuilding tribal societies, implementing written laws, and adapting to the changing political circumstances of the times. Few federally-recognized Tribes resisted the new "IRA-Constitution" government structure and there is great similarity in the adopted tribal constitutions across Indian Country. Notable non-IRA Tribes are the Navajo Nation, the Sisseton-Wahpeton Oyate, and the Confederated Tribes of the Colville Reservation. The Oklahoma Indian Welfare Act of 1936, 25 U.S.C. § 501 et seq., provided the Tribes in Oklahoma the same opportunity to organize under the tribal constitution model. For Alaska Natives, the Alaska Reorganization Act of 1936, 49 Stat. 1250, also extended the general provisions of the IRA to the Alaska Native villages. Tribal constitutions often contain clauses that provide approval by the U.S. Secretary of the Interior or even the President of the United States to amend the tribal constitution.

With the re-emergence of tribal governmental authority, political backlash led to a change in U.S. policy embodied in the termination era. Through House Resolution No. 108 of the U.S. Congress, the policy goal of withdrawing federal recognition of Tribal Nations and the "Indian" status of tribal citizens began in 1953. The justification for termination of federal recognition was to allow Indian people to join the mainstream U.S. society and abolish the separate status of reservation Indians. The impact of the termination era on tribal sovereignty was severe as the U.S. government's actions allowed state and county assertions of jurisdiction over territories no longer considered Indian Country. Furthermore, loss of federal recognition ended individual eligibility for treaty-guaranteed health, education and other benefits. Several national tribal leadership associations were formed in resistance to the U.S. termination policy, such as the regional Tribal Chairman's associations and the National Congress of American Indians.

Since the late 1960s, the U.S. Indian policy era has been heralded as the Indian self-determination era. President Richard Nixon in his special address on Indian affairs to the U.S. Congress on July 8, 1970 announced his intention to abandon the termination policy in Indian affairs and move towards a policy of self-determination through tribal decision-making over Indian affairs. This is the present policy of U.S. Indian affairs and the one in which tribal governments continue to operate and rebuild tribal communities with the assistance of the U.S. government.

B. Civil Jurisdiction in Indian Country

As sovereigns, tribal governments have an obligation to tribal citizenry and visitors to the tribal territory to provide basic services for health, education, safety, transportation routes, communication networks, support for commerce, employment opportunities, and forums to resolve disputes. All of these governmental roles fall within the civil jurisdiction of the tribal government.

1. Tribal Councils, Laws and Courts

Under tribal constitutions, the Tribal Council serves as the governing body over the executive, legislative and judicial functions of the Tribe. The original template tribal constitutions did not provide for three separate branches of government, rather all three functions were consolidated in the elected Tribal Council. Amendments to tribal constitutions have occurred providing for tribal judge elections, deleting approval authority by the Secretary of the Interior over tribal decision-making power, and broadening the blood quantum qualifications for tribal citizenship.

Tribal constitutions may vary in the number of seats on the Tribal Council and whether council members are elected from specific political districts or at-large by vote of the entire tribal citizenry. Qualifications for elected office and the election process are governed by the tribal election commission with most tribal constitutions requiring a certification of election results by the outgoing Tribal Council. Terms of office for tribal council members are usually set at either two, three or four year terms with some Tribes providing for staggered terms to provide continuity on government projects from year to year. There are some tribal constitutions that provide for a meeting of all tribal citizenry in a General Council annual or bi-annual session with the authority, based upon a quorum present, to veto or modify actions of the Tribal Council. Each Tribe's governing documents should be reviewed prior to any dealings with the tribal government to understand the particular governance structure of the Tribal Nation.

The Tribal Council carries forth the legislative function by creating the laws of the Tribe along with adopting revisions and amendments to those laws. In its executive function, the Tribal Council provides enforcement of the tribal laws through supervision of all governmental departments, services, contracts, and programs. The body of tribal laws is commonly called the Tribal Code. Due to the common needs of tribal governments, Tribal Councils may choose to model new laws on those of other Tribes and revise existing laws to better suit the needs of the particular Tribe. Tribal attorneys often work closely with Tribal Councils in developing new laws, providing drafting services, and researching legal issues involved.

As tribal government seeks to implement new policies, tribal laws are developed to govern the efforts. For example, tribal gaming businesses are subject to specific federal laws that required tribal legislation governing tribal gaming operations in line with minimum federal regulatory standards. To keep pace with governmental goals and federal requirements, Tribal Councils must devote considerable time to legislative matters. Tribal laws may be comprehensive code sections, such as an environmental standards code, or isolated specific laws, such as declaring a tribal holiday commemorating a historic treaty council.

Tribal laws become subject to judicial interpretation when parties seek to resolve disputes in tribal courts. The authority of tribal courts to resolve cases is referred to as the court's adjudicative authority. Tribal courts may exercise only civil adjudicative authority or may have both criminal and civil adjudicative authority. Tribal judges and court personnel often experience high volumes of civil cases on court dockets while dealing with issues of being underfunded, lack of adequate facilities and technology, and, at times, external pressure by tribal politicians, tribal citizenry, or non-tribal citizens.

In the civil litigation context, tribal court decision archives are important to determine how a court has ruled on any previous similar legal issue. Accessing tribal court archives usually requires the assistance of tribal court clerks and staff. In recent years, online access to tribal laws, court decisions, and regulations has increased through legal information service providers, however, a full range of on-line access is still limited to a handful of Tribes with the resources to provide both historical archives and newly updated legal information. As resources become available, the current trend is towards archiving tribal court decisions for retrievable purposes to aid attorneys and judges in the tribal court systems. Tribal court staff members are often highly knowledgeable on the tribal court system they serve and are key to working competently within the system.

Tribal judges may serve for an appointed time under a contract with the tribal government and be present for court hearings on designated days per month. Judges may also be elected for a set term by the entire tribal citizenry and then subject to re-election every term on a more permanent basis. Formal legal training has become a norm for serving in a tribal judge position in recent years. In some tribal courts, lay judges may preside only over certain types of cases or may have the same status as law-trained judges to hear all types of cases before the court. For those tribal court systems which include an appeals court, the common procedure is to have a list of qualified appellate judges to call upon when an appeal is filed. The appeals court may consist of one appellate judge per appeal or a panel of three or more judges to rule on an appeal. Tribal judicial associations for specific regions may be joined by local Tribes to provide an appellate court of neutral decision-makers. Examples of these types of associations include the Northern Plains Intertribal Court of Appeals and the Southwest Intertribal Court of Appeals. Practitioners of tribal law, law professors in the field and judges of other court systems may all serve as appellate judges in tribal court systems.

Court dockets with a wide variety of cases may require several tribal judges with each assigned to particular types of cases. For example, a tribal judge may oversee only cases on the domestic issues docket concerning family matters, such as marriages, divorces, child custody and support, guardianships, and probate matters. In other court systems, the tribal judge will oversee all matters before the court in all areas of tribal law. As with other court systems, tribal laws provide the civil procedure for litigants. Practitioners in a tribal court system are expected to become familiar with the rules of civil procedure prior to filing a case in tribal court.

2. Federal Limitations on Tribal Adjudicative Authority

In the criminal jurisdiction context, the U.S. Supreme Court has held that there is no tribal criminal jurisdiction over non-Indians who commit crimes in the tribal territory. In the civil jurisdiction context, the U.S. Supreme Court has imposed limitations that will be discussed in this section. A series of U.S. Supreme Court decisions must be taken into consideration to determine whether a tribal court has adjudicatory authority over civil cases when a non-member/non-Indian is a party. The starting point for an analysis of a Tribe's civil jurisdiction begins with inherent tribal jurisdiction within the tribal territory. Through federal court decisions, the next steps are to determine: whether each party to the litigation in tribal court is a tribal citizen, what the status of the land is where the cause of action arose, and what conduct is at issue in the case.

The foundational federal case on tribal civil jurisdiction limitations is *Montana v. United States*, 450 U.S. 544 (1981). The U.S. Supreme Court set out a general principle that inherent tribal civil authority does not extend over activities by non-members subject to two exceptions. From this case, the *Montana* test was formed with two prongs to determine tribal court civil adjudicatory jurisdiction over non-members. The first prong is whether the non-member entered into "consensual relationships with the [T]ribe or its members through commercial dealing, contracts or other arrangements." 450 U.S. at 565. This is referred to as the "consensual relations" prong. If this first prong is met, then the tribal court has civil authority over the case and the non-member for the conduct that gave rise to the litigation.

The second prong of the *Montana* test is whether the conduct of the non-Indian/non-member, on land within the tribal territory, "threatens or has some direct effect on the political integrity, the economic security, or the health or welfare of the [T]ribe." 450 U.S. 566. This is referred to as the "direct effects" prong. If this prong is met, then the tribal court may exercise civil authority over the case and the non-member for the conduct that created the cause of action for the litigation.

The *Montana* test's two prongs, "consensual relations" and "direct effects," are to be applied to civil actions in tribal courts where a non-member is a defendant in the case. In another series of cases, the U.S. Supreme Court held that the tribal court is the proper forum to first decide whether it has civil jurisdiction before a non-member can seek to challenge tribal jurisdiction in a federal court. In *National Farmers Union v. Crow Tribe*, 471 U.S. 845 (1985), the Court held that a non-member must exhaust all tribal remedies before challenging tribal court jurisdiction in a federal court. This is referred to as the "tribal exhaustion doctrine" which requires a challenging party to receive final judgment at all levels of the tribal court system raising the issue of whether tribal civil adjudicatory authority is proper before the party can file suit in federal court to bring a challenge to tribal court authority. The Court reasoned that there was a federal question involved when a party challenged tribal court authority which gave the federal courts jurisdiction to ultimately determine the matter once tribal remedies were exhausted.

In *National Farmers Union*, the Court provided three exceptions to the application of the tribal exhaustion doctrine. First, the Court stated a challenging party need not exhaust all levels of tribal court review prior to filing in federal court if the assertion of tribal jurisdiction "is motivated by a desire to harass or conducted in bad faith." Second, the doctrine will not apply "where the action is patently violative of express jurisdictional prohibitions." Third, the challenging party can file in federal court without exhaustion of tribal remedies "where exhaustion would be futile because of the lack of an adequate opportunity to challenge the court's jurisdiction." 471 U.S. at 856 fn. 21.

Two U.S. Supreme Court cases following the *National Farmers Union* case sharpened the tribal exhaustion doctrine's application for tribal court civil cases. In *Iowa Mutual Insurance Company v. LaPlante*, 480 U.S. 9 (1987), the Court stated that the tribal exhaustion doctrine was operative when a non-member filed suit in federal court on a diversity of citizenship basis at the same time a tribal court case was in process over the matter. The Court rejected the challenging party's assertion that the tribal court was incompetent and there-fore, the tribal exhaustion doctrine should not apply. This case upheld the tribal exhaustion doctrine and required the non-member to go through all lev-els of the tribal judicial system before filing a case in federal court challenging the tribal court's authority.

Finally, in *Strate v. A-1 Contractors*, 520 U.S. 438 (1997), the Court deter-mined that a civil action brought in tribal court which involved a collision be-tween a truck and a car both driven by non-members which occurred on land not considered within the tribal status was outside of the tribal civil adjudica-tory authority. The Court further stated that the tribal exhaustion doctrine did not apply to this case based upon the reasoning that exhaustion would "serve no purpose other than delay," 520 U.S. at 459 fn. 14. In finding that the tribal court lacked adjudicatory authority in the case, the Court stated that the *Montana* test exceptions were not met in this personal injury case because the conduct by the defendant non-member did not meet either the consensual re-lations or the direct effects prong.

In sum, inherent tribal civil authority has been limited by federal court deci-sions when that authority is applied to non-members on non-tribal lands within tribal boundaries. Tribal Nations retain civil jurisdiction over non-members who enter into consensual relations with the Tribe or its tribal members and when a non-member's conduct has a direct effect on the Tribe. Tribal courts have the authority to determine the extent of their civil jurisdiction before a challenge can be brought into federal court under the tribal exhaustion doctrine.

C. Regulatory Authority in
Indian Country

As a general rule, Tribal Nations retain inherent regulatory authority within Indian Country. This inherent authority has been discussed at length in fed-eral court decisions when states have sought to regulate within Indian Coun-try. The major court decisions and tension between tribal and state regulatory jurisdiction will be discussed in this section. In specific areas, such as meeting federal environmental standards, federal regulatory authority is the default when tribal government does not provide regulatory authority. Additionally, the BIA has regulatory authority in certain matters based on trust land status and federal service delivery in Indian Country. When a question arises over regulatory authority in Indian Country, tribal government should be the first point of inquiry to determine the proper authority for a regulatory issue.

1. Tribal Law and Administrative Bodies

As tribal governments have established governmental services and agencies to administer those services, dispute resolution processes have been necessary outgrowths as part of the delivery of services in the tribal territory. A foundational service provided by tribal government is employment within its branches. The majority of Tribes have formal personnel policies and employment dispute resolution processes. Best practices for the exercise of tribal regulatory authority include: allowing comment periods prior to the adoption of new regulations or policies; clear and concise written regulations/policies readily available to those impacted; and non-interference on the political level of administrative agency actions. Agency administrative action is at its most effective when regulations and policies are well-known, easily understood, and consistently followed.

Dispute resolution processes in the regulatory context can range from an immediate petition to the Tribal Council for hearing to a multi-tiered review panel process allowing an appeal to the tribal court. Tribal Nations have the option of establishing subject matter specific dispute resolution forums. For example, the Prairie Band Potawatomi Nation has created a forum, the Employment Disputes Tribunal, with five individuals as magistrates appointed by both the Tribal Council and tribal government employees for resolving employment issues. Another route is for the Tribal Council to provide dispute resolution mechanisms in the same set of tribal laws establishing the administrative agency as a delegation to that agency.

Many Tribal Nations have created Tribal Employment Rights Offices (TEROs) that serve a variety of administrative functions. A primary role of the TEROs is to maintain the tribal preference status in employment and government contracting under tribal law. The enforcement of the tribal preference status requires an administrative oversight body to provide lists of eligible tribally-owned businesses when opportunities arise within the tribal territory. TEROs may also provide lists of skilled tribal workers available for temporary hire or for hire on projects as subcontractors. Tribal law may provide that the TEROs exercise the ability to assess sanctions and fines for non-compliance by employers and contractors doing business with tribal government. On the national level, the

Council for Tribal Employment Rights holds annual meetings to provide updates on tribal and federal legislation developments; to provide a networking opportunity among TEROs; and to exchange information on opportunities for tribal employment.

For the related areas of commercial activity and contracting, Tribal Councils have commonly created tribal revenue and taxation departments to administer business licenses within the tribal jurisdiction and to collect business-related taxes. With the development of tribal gaming enterprises, Tribal Nations put in place tribal gaming laws and regulations on a full-scale level for almost every aspect of the gaming operations. The chief regulatory agency for tribal gaming is often called the tribal gaming commission which operates under a delegation of authority from tribal government to enforce tribal gaming laws and establish regulations as needed for the lawful and efficient performance of the tribal business.

Domestic relations services are part of the purpose of tribal government. Providing for the health, education and welfare of the tribal citizenship is at the forefront of tribal governmental priorities. Tribal Nations have put time and energy into the creation of child support enforcement offices, child protection and social work services, domestic violence prevention agencies, and elder community centers. Programs, agencies, and offices working in the domestic service delivery sector require dispute resolution processes and proper regulations in determining service eligibility, level of service provisions, and resolving service-related issues.

A major undertaking of most tribal governments is to provide residential homes and planned neighborhoods for tribal citizens. U.S. governmental grant funding has served as the historical method of providing tribal housing. Through the Native American Housing Assistance and Self-Determination Act (NA-HASDA) of 1996, tribal governments had the opportunity to receive direct block grant funding and utilize a guaranteed loan program from the U.S. Department of Housing and Urban Development (HUD) to provide housing in tribal communities. The work of tribal housing departments involves regulatory authority over financing and implementing the legal obligations imposed by HUD. Additionally, tribal laws and regulations are necessary to establish tenant responsibilities and obligations. Within tribal community areas, tribal regulatory authority may be exerted for neighborhood quality of life standards such as enforcement of residential waste restrictions or animal control policies.

In conjunction with maintaining tribal residential areas, tribal governments have engaged in community planning efforts and often have delegated authority to land use and planning agencies to zone tribal land areas for specific uses. Regulations may govern a land use permitting process or utility construction in a newly zoned area. Stewardship of tribal lands has led to environmental protection legislation and oversight agencies. Tribal environmental departments may have regulations on a wide-variety of environmental standards, such as air quality, emission controls, water quality, instream flow standards for tribal waterways, ceremonial sites use, and solid waste disposal regulations.

Traditional tribal activities of hunting, fishing and gathering may now require detailed regulations due to negotiations with federal and state governments to continue to exercise reserved rights off-reservation and on-reservation. Tribal fishery and hunting departments manage permit processes for quantity and type of fish or game. Fines and equipment confiscation may be administered by departmental personnel in enforcing regulations. Seasonal limitations may be established in regulations with violators subject to penalties under tribal law. These types of regulations may be likened to the historic policies of clans tasked with the authority to oversee fishing, hunting and gathering times of the tribal community.

One more area worth noting that is common to most tribal governments as a matter of regulatory authority is the administration of tribal elections. The general procedures governing tribal elections may be contained in the tribal constitution with a provision allowing for the creation of an election board to implement and add to those general directives. Election regulations usually detail candidate eligibility requirements, voter eligibility, availability of absentee voting and under what circumstances, the review of election board determinations, and other aspects related to electing tribal representatives. Because the election of tribal leadership is at the heart of tribal government, it is common for an appeal of an election board determination to be fast-tracked in the tribal court to meet timing deadlines in the election process.

In sum, tribal regulatory authority is extensive and covers a wide range of governmental services, processes, and responsibilities. Rule-making in Indian Country is an on-going activity of tribal agencies and offices to implement new tribal laws, to meet federal statutory provisions, and to address areas of concern raised by those residing in the tribal community. For the safe and effective functioning of tribal communities, tribal government often delegates rule-making authority to the agencies, boards, and offices directly serving the community as the firsthand experts on the needed regulations.

2. BIA Administration in Indian Country

As part of the trust responsibility to Indian Country, the U.S. federal agency directly delivering treaty and agreement guaranteed services is the Bureau of Indian Affairs (BIA) within the U.S. Department of the Interior. The regulations created to implement federal Indian programs, policies, and responsibilities are contained in the Code of Federal Regulations in Title 25 — Indians Chapter I Bureau of Indian Affairs, Department of the Interior. This extensive set of regulations governs the implementation of federal laws and policies providing processes and standards to be met.

A quick survey of the regulations in 25 C.F.R. Chapter I includes regulations concerning: Indian Country law enforcement (25 C.F.R. § 12); Probates of Indian estates (25 C.F.R. § 15); Federal schools for Indians (25 C.F.R. § 31); Preparation of rolls of Indians (25 C.F.R. § 61); Trust funds for tribes and individual Indians (25 C.F.R. § 115); and many other subjects of federal administration. Thus, the BIA has numerous regulations in place that affect the daily operation of federal and tribal services for tribal governments and individual tribal citizens.

Title 25 of the Code of Federal Regulations contains several other chapters that all pertain to federal Indian policy and service delivery. Chapter II provides regulations for the Department of Interior's oversight of the Indian Arts and Crafts Board. Chapter III contains the regulations issued by the National Indian Gaming Commission to implement the Indian Gaming Regulatory Act, 25 U.S.C. § 2701 et seq. In Chapter IV, the regulations are set forth for the specific federal policy carried out by the Navajo and Hopi Relocation Office.

Title 25 Chapter V of the Code of Federal Regulations implements a federal policy known as "Indian self-determination" passed into federal legislation in 1975. Under the Indian Self-Determination and Education Assistance Act, 25 U.S.C. § 450, many of the federal programs administered specifically to serve tribal populations became available for tribal government administration upon entering into a contract between the BIA and the tribal government. These contracts are popularly called "638 contracts" derived from the title of Public Law 93-638, as the bill was known when enacted into federal law. The regulations contained in Chapter V provide the means and processes through which a Tribal Nation applies for administration of a particular federal program, such as a 638 contract for operation of Tribal Court services. Tribal Nations must provide detailed documentation of the program operation, performance standards, and budget planning to receive funding and approval of the 638 contract. At regular intervals, the Tribal Nation is responsible for submitting performance and financial reports to the BIA for continuation of the 638 contract.

Title 25 Chapter VI includes the regulations that accompany the amendments to the Indian Self-Determination and Assistance Act. A provision of the Act included an initial pilot project called "Indian Self-Governance." The second set of regulations in Chapter VI implement the full-scale Indian Self-

Governance provisions which allow a Tribal Nation to submit a package of programs for contracting and implementation and receive funding for the entire package without adhering to in-depth reporting requirements to the BIA per program. In response to the Indian Self-Governance initiative, the Indian Health Service (IHS), for example, created the Office of Tribal Self-Governance which is responsible for a national program to provide information and technical assistance to tribal governments and organizations in support of IHS Self-Governance activities.

The final chapter of Title 25 is Chapter VII containing the regulations derived from the Office of Special Trustee within the Department of the Interior implementing the American Indian Trust Fund Management Reform Act of 1994, 25 U.S.C. § 4001 et seq. These regulations govern technical assistance to tribal governments who may wish to participate in the management of trust funds or remove funds from the U.S. government trust to invest in compliance with federal regulations.

In the daily functioning of tribal government, the regulations contained in Title 25 of the Code of Federal Regulations have a significant role. In this set of regulations, the appeals processes for BIA determinations that impose important consequences on tribal government action are set forth. The delivery of federally-guaranteed services to tribal populations and governments are regulated within this title of the Code of Federal Regulations. Practitioners in Indian Country working on behalf of Tribal Nations or individual tribal citizens must have a working knowledge of pertinent regulations contained in Title 25 for many of the land, education, health and welfare issues within tribal communities.

Checkpoints

- Tribal governance is traditionally based upon clan systems and kinship networks that require adherence to high level standards of conduct. With the influence of the U.S., the majority of tribal governance systems have shifted toward constitutionally based governments.

- Tribal Courts resolve disputes involving civil laws. Non-tribal members have certain procedural avenues to challenge the civil adjudicatory authority of Tribal Courts when actions arise on certain lands within tribal boundaries.

- Tribal governments have various administrative agencies and offices to carry out civil regulatory functions, such as: tax offices, personnel agencies, and departments of fishing and hunting.

- Many tribal social services are guaranteed under treaty provisions with the U.S. government. These guaranteed services are administered by federal agencies, but may be contracted and operated by tribal governments.

Chapter 5

Tribal Business, Industries and Best Commercial Practices

Roadmap

- Learn about the rich tribal history of kinship commercial networks that are being resurrected through contemporary markets.

- Learn that tribal-government owned businesses are the norm in Indian Country. Tribal economic development is a high priority to provide a better quality of life in tribal communities.

- Understand the primary relationship between Europeans and Tribal Nations was based on commerce. The U.S. Constitution contains the Indian Commerce Clause placing regulatory authority as a matter of congressional responsibility.

- Understand the types of economic incentive programs enacted in federal Indian law to support tribal economic development.

- Know the best practices for tribal commercial practices.

This chapter addresses tribal governmental economic development, highlights the federal incentives for tribal-government owned business, and offers general principles of best commercial practices in tribal communities. According to the report issued in 2003 by the U.S. Commission on Civil Rights, *A Quiet Crisis: Federal Funding and Unmet Needs in Indian Country,* Native Americans continue to suffer from intergenerational poverty. From pages 34 and 35 of the report:

> Native Americans have a lower life expectancy — nearly six years less — and higher disease occurrence than other racial/ethnic groups. Roughly 13 percent of Native American deaths occur among those under the age of 25, a rate three times more than that of the total U.S. population. Native American youth are more than twice as likely to commit suicide, and nearly 70 percent of all suicidal acts in Indian Country involve alcohol. Native Americans are 670 percent more likely to die

from alcoholism, 650 percent more likely to die from tuberculosis, 318 percent more likely to die from diabetes, and 204 percent more likely to suffer accidental death when compared with other groups. These disparities exist because of disproportionate poverty, poor education, cultural differences, and the absence of adequate health service delivery in most Native communities.

Tribal economic development is a high priority for tribal leadership to alleviate these disparities occurring in tribal communities. Economic development is particularly important because tribal governments do not enjoy the same tax base as federal, state, and other local governments.

A. Historical Tribal Trade Practices

Tribal commercial activity has been on-going since time immemorial. Tribal Nations and peoples have established well-traveled trade routes that became the paved highways connecting the United States in mid-North America. Prior to European settlements in the Western Hemisphere, Tribal Nations had far-reaching commercial relationships with each other from the tip of North America to the southernmost point of South America. As Europeans expanded into tribal territories, the first relationships between Tribes and Europeans were centered on commercial exchange which led to mutual alliances, intermarriage, cross-cultural exchanges and, at times, warfare.

Historical trading practices between tribal peoples in mid-North America were based upon a worldview of kinship. Engaging in trade with relatives required fair dealing, quality exchanges, and a sense of obligation beyond the trade transaction. These concepts were carried over to trade relationships with the newcomers to tribal lands, namely the French, Spanish, Russians, Dutch, and British, depending on geographical location. From the late 1500s until the late 1700s, Europeans established trading posts and colonies in mid-North America under the authority of religious orders and monarchies in Europe. Tribal alliances were sought by the Europeans seeking beneficial trading relationships to export goods back to Europe.

The fur trade for European export and the metal weaponry and metal implement trade for Tribal Nation citizenry formed the basis of initial trading exchanges. The British sought formal agreements to form tribal alliances with large Tribal Nations in the northeastern region of North America. This custom of international treaty-making was similar to the unions and confederacies entered into between Tribal Nations as part of enlarging kinship and trade networks.

1. U.S. Policy on Commerce with Tribes

Beginning with the revolt by the British colonies along the eastern seaboard of mid-North America, a permanent settlement of Euro-Americans was established as the newly formed United States of America. As the U.S. government was organized, the importance of commerce with Tribal Nations became incorporated in first the Articles of Confederation and later, in the U.S. Constitution. Article 1, section 8 of the U.S. Constitution empowers the U.S. Congress as follows: "To regulate Commerce with foreign Nations, and among the several States, and with the Indian Tribes." The U.S. Congress implemented legislation to exercise this authority with Tribal Nations soon thereafter.

2. U.S. Trade and Intercourse Acts

In the first set of statutes enacted by the United States, the Trade and Intercourse Act of 1790, 1 stat. 137 (July 22, 1790) was included and is commonly referred to as the "Non-Intercourse Act." As the original Act was set to expire, Congress passed re-enactments and in 1834, 25 U.S.C. §177, the expiration provision was eliminated, so the Act remains federal law. The purpose of the Act was to authorize the purchase of Indian lands exclusively by the U.S. federal government. Any other purchases would be violations of the federal law and subject a violator to a penalty of $1000. By creating a federal law that made the federal government the only legally recognized purchaser of tribal lands, the threat of land speculators or other countries gaining territory in mid-North America was addressed. This restriction on the right to sell land imposed upon tribal governments remains in effect. Thus, under present federal Indian law, the U.S. government is the sole entity entitled to purchase land from tribal governments within the borders of the U.S. This has barred tribal governments from entering into the real estate markets of the U.S. when lands are tribally-owned.

3. Indian Trader Licensing

Regulation of commerce included federal statutes and regulations specifying requirements to license Indian traders within tribal territories. The Commissioner of Indian Affairs in 1876 was empowered to appoint licensed traders governed by federal regulations, 25 U.S.C. §261. Indian traders may be licensed up to a period of 25 years and must meet the requirements under the federal regulations to conduct business on Indian reservations, 25 C.F.R. § 140.11. Anecdotal accounts have been handed down in many tribal communities of unethical trading post owners who extended credit to Indian families and then presented a statement of debts to the local Indian agent and thereby, received the family's share of treaty payments directly. The federal regulations prohibit such conduct along with the sale of liquor and drugs by Indian traders, 25 C.F.R. §§ 140.23, 140.18, and 140.19.

4. Federal "Buy Indian Act" and the Indian Arts and Crafts Board

The U.S. Congress passed in 1908 a law encouraging the Secretary of the Interior to employ Indian labor and purchase products from American Indians "on the open market" and when "practicable," 25 U.S.C. § 47. This law is known as the "Buy Indian Act." In addition to this law, another federal statute established the Indian Arts and Craft Board in 1935 within the Department of the Interior to promote the marketing of products created by American Indians as beneficial for their economic welfare, 25 U.S.C. § 305.

To ensure that the marketplace acknowledged genuinely created art and crafts from tribal members, federal criminal statutes provide penalties for fraudulent claims that items are "Indian-made." Under the Indian Arts and Crafts Act of 1990, offering, displaying for sale or selling an item and misrepresenting that it is "Indian produced, an Indian product, or the product of a particular Indian or Indian tribe or Indian arts and crafts organization" is unlawful, 18 U.S.C. § 1159(a). Both federally-recognized and state-recognized Indian tribes and their members are included in the definitions section of the law, 18 U.S.C. § 1159(c)(3). The penalties under this law increase for subsequent offenses. Individuals and businesses falsely marketing goods as Indian-produced are subject to fines and/or incarceration, 18 U.S.C. § 1159(b). In addition, a civil action for monetary damages may be brought by the U.S. Attorney General upon recommendation of the Secretary of the Interior, the Indian Arts and Crafts Board, a tribal government, an individual Indian artisan, or an association of Indian artists against a violator of the Indian Arts and Crafts Act, 25 U.S.C. § 305(e). Any amounts recovered from the violator are awarded to the tribal government, tribal individual or arts association on whose behalf the action was filed.

These laws are examples of the federal government's role from the early 1900s to the present in promoting American Indian services, products, and arts. Through the Indian Arts and Crafts Act, the U.S. has a responsibility to protect the authenticity of "Indian-made" products.

B. Contemporary Tribal Commerce

The contemporary growth of tribal commerce traces back to the policy shift in U.S. Indian affairs by the 1930s. Prior to this time, few Tribal Nations were able to meet basic sustenance needs for tribal peoples. Due to the allotment of tribal lands, the territorial harvesting of wild rice, corn, squash, berries and other natural foodstuffs was disrupted, with movement limited to small parcels of individually-owned allotments. Hunting and fishing seasons were also severely limited or altogether prohibited by Indian agents at the same time. As intergenerational poverty set in for tribal peoples, an outcry from concerned organizations and federal officials led to the ushering in of new federal legislation intended to lessen federal control over tribal lands and tribal governments.

1. Tribal Constitutions and Federal Loan Funds

As part of the new deal legislation in the 1930s, the Indian Reorganization Act (IRA) of 1934 signaled a return to proactive tribal government and more autonomy from the Bureau of Indian Affairs. This was particularly true in the business realm for tribal governments. Specifically, the IRA provided a process for adopting a tribal constitution that contained governmental powers to enter into contracts, handle business affairs and interact with the federal government, 25 U.S.C. §476(e). This portion of the law was originally enacted as section 16 recognizing the authority of tribal governments to establish tribal laws to form business corporations. Under 25 U.S.C. §477, Tribal Nations had the opportunity to seek a federal charter incorporating a business owned by the tribal government. The federally-chartered tribal corporations operating under this provision are often referred to as section 17 corporations. After a tribal corporation receives approval for a federal charter, the charter remains in effect unless revoked by an act of Congress. An excellent resource detailing tribal corporations and businesses across the country is Tiller's Guide to Indian Country: Economic Profiles of American Indian Reservations (BowArrow Publishing, 2006 ed.) by Dr. Veronica Tiller.

To assist tribal business entities entering into the U.S. economy, the IRA established a federal revolving loan fund, 25 U.S.C. §470. In 1961, the federal law was amended to increase the federal appropriation into the revolving fund from $10 million to $20 million. In 1974, Congress consolidated monies from various federal law provisions and consolidated funds into one general Indian Revolving Loan Fund available to both tribal governments and individuals, 25 U.S.C. §1461. The Secretary of the Interior is vested with the authority to receive loan applications by Indian organizations, corporations and individuals. The two standards under the applicable statute are: 1) "there is a reasonable prospect of repayment" from the loan applicants and 2) the loan applicants are "unable to obtain financing from other sources on reasonable terms and conditions," 25 U.S.C. § 1463. The federal regulations governing direct federal loans to Indian entities and individuals are at 25 C.F.R. § 101.

2. Tribal-Government Owned Corporations, Alaska Native Corporations, and Native Hawaiian Organizations

Many Tribal Nations have adopted corporation and business entities law provisions or codes. These tribal laws provide the process for organizing a business entity, registering the business with the tribal government, and the responsibilities and tax liabilities of the business entity. For example, the Dry Creek Rancheria Band of Pomo Indians Business Code Title 3 Corporations and Tribal Entities established a Tribal Department of Commerce to receive applications for incorporation and to issue certificates of incorporation upon approval of a business entity, Title 3 Section 5(B).

a. Establishment and Features of Tribally-Owned Corporations

When the tribal government establishes a tribal corporation under tribal laws, the corporation operates differently than one formed under state law. The tribal corporation owned by the tribal government is governed by the tribal legislative acts primarily, although the Tribal Council, or tribal legislative branch, may appoint a Board of Directors which would report back to the Council on matters relating to the corporation. Typically, no stocks or shares would issue from this type of corporation to individual tribal citizens. In a few instances, tribal-government owned corporations have issued one share to each member of the Tribal Council during their term of office. Tribal citizens would indirectly influence the corporation's operation through their power to elect those who serve on the Tribal Council. Profits from tribal corporations are available to return to the tribal government, to be reinvested in the corporation, or to fund specific programs as determined by the Tribal Council.

Tribal governments may seek to purchase ownership interests in corporations formed under state laws or to establish corporations under state law. Such state law-created business entities do not enjoy tribal sovereign immunity and are subject to state regulation and taxation. The more common practice is for tribal governments to operate corporations formed under tribal law.

Tribal corporations formed under tribal authority as recognized in section 16 of the IRA enjoy tribal sovereign immunity unless such immunity is ex-

Prairie Band Potawatomi Signs. Photo credit Ramona Nozhackum.

pressly waived by the corporation. This prevents the corporation from being sued without its consent. As a practical matter, tribal corporations often waive tribal sovereign immunity to do business with other entities and set out in contracts the process for dispute resolution and the proper court to resolve litigation that arises from the business interaction.

Section 17 tribal corporations under federal charters must be approved by the Secretary of the Interior. These federal charters may include a "sue and be sued" clause for dispute resolution purposes. At least one state court has interpreted the "sue and be sued" clause of a section 17 corporation as permitting the corporation to be sued to the full extent of the corporate assets, thus excluding the tribal government's assets. In the *S. Unique, Ltd. v. Gila River Pima-Maricopa Indian Community* case, the Arizona Court of Appeals opined that the section 17 corporate defendant could be sued in Arizona state courts due to the corporate charter's "sue and be sued" clause along with the provision that suit could be brought "in courts of competent jurisdiction within the United States," 674 P.2d 1376, 1383 (Ariz. Ct. App. 1983).

For Tribal Nations in Oklahoma, the Oklahoma Indian Welfare Act (OIWA) of 1936 provided similar key features found in the Indian Reorganization Act.

The OIWA contains one section that authorized both adoption of tribal constitutions and issuance of federal corporate charters to Oklahoma Tribes, 25 U.S.C. § 503. The next section of the OIWA provides for another business structure, the cooperative association, 25 U.S.C. § 504. "Any ten or more Indians, as determined by the official tribal rolls, or Indian descendants of such enrolled members, or Indians as defined in the Act of June 18, 1934 [IRA, 25 U.S.C. § 461 et seq.], who reside within the State of Oklahoma in convenient proximity to each other may receive from the Secretary of the Interior a charter as a local cooperative association for any one or more of the following purposes: Credit administration, production, marketing, consumers' protection or land management." *Id.* Further, the cooperative association once organized may be dissolved by a majority vote of the membership. An organized cooperative association was held to be available to legal action in state court and any court filings were to also be served on the Secretary of the Interior to allow intervention in the suit or removal to federal court, 25 U.S.C. § 505.

As a general matter, Tribal Nations enjoy sovereign immunity from lawsuits filed without the consent of the tribal government. This was upheld in the 1998 U.S. Supreme Court decision, *Kiowa Tribe of Oklahoma v. Manufacturing Technologies, Inc.,* 523 U.S. 751, holding that the Tribe could not be brought into an Oklahoma state court on a loan repayment issue without tribal consent to the state court's jurisdiction. Following this line of cases from the U.S. Supreme Court, the power of the doctrine of tribal sovereign immunity for a tribal government's off-reservation business activities was upheld in *Ogden v. Iowa Tribe of Kansas and Nebraska,* 250 S.W.3d 822, 825 (Mo. Ct. App. 2008), when a former employee brought suit against the tribal government in a Missouri state court. The case was dismissed on sovereign immunity grounds and the Missouri Court of Appeals affirmed.

In 2001 the U.S. Supreme Court broadly interpreted waiver of tribal sovereign immunity in the decision, *C & L Enterprises, Inc. v. Citizen Band of Potawatomi Indian Tribe of Oklahoma,* 532 U.S. 411. In that case the Tribe entered into a contract that contained a clause authorizing arbitration for dispute resolution and that the arbitration judgment could be filed in "any court having jurisdiction." A dispute went to arbitration with the arbitration judgment filed subsequently in Oklahoma state court and the Tribe objected on sovereign immunity grounds to the authority of the state court, 532 U.S. at 415. In its decision, the U.S. Supreme Court found that by entering into the contract with the wording contained in the arbitration clause the Tribe had consented to a waiver of tribal sovereign immunity when the arbitration award was filed in state court for enforcement, 532 U.S. at 420. Thus, contract wording is important to put all parties on notice of what form of dispute resolution is agreed upon and, if litigation ensues, what court(s) will have authority to hear the case.

b. Establishment and Features of Alaska Native Corporations

Pursuant to the passage of the Alaska Native Claims Settlement Act (ANCSA) of 1971, 43 U.S.C. § 1601, et seq., Alaska Native Corporations were authorized to be organized under Alaska state law as the entities receiving monetary and land settlements in exchange for the release of title and aboriginal claims in the state. Thirteen regional Alaska Native Corporations (ANCs) were authorized under the federal law, 43 U.S.C. § 1606. In addition, over 200 Alaska Native Village Corporations were also formed from the original village communities as economic entities under state law. Under the ANCSA, membership rolls were established by the Secretary of the Interior for eligible Alaska Natives to claim compensation for the extinguishment of aboriginal title, 43 U.S.C. § 1604.

With the establishment of the regional ANCs, federal law provided for an initial issuance of 100 shares of common stock to each Alaska Native eligible in the regional ANC based upon the federal membership rolls, 43 U.S.C. § 1606(g). Amendments to the ANCSA have provided that additional shares could be issued for Alaska Natives who were born after 1971 upon affirmative vote from current shareholders. ANCSA also places restrictions on selling of the corporate shares, 43 U.S.C. § 1606(h)(1)(B). Finally, shares that are passed from original Alaska Native shareholders to non-Natives do not have voting rights attached, 43 U.S.C. § 1606(h)(2)(C).

Alaska Native Corporations are dissimilar to tribally-owned corporations because ANCs are organized under Alaska state law with all of the state regulations, state taxes, and state requirements attaching to the entities as state businesses. ANCs are specialized under federal law in the shareholder provisions limiting voting rights to eligible Alaska Natives and placing restrictions on alienation as described in the ANCSA.

c. Tribal Corporations, ANCs, Native Hawaiian Organizations and the Federal SBA Native 8(a) Program

Under the provisions of Section 16 and 17 of the 1934 Indian Reorganization Act, tribal-government owned corporations were established to provide a foundation for rebuilding tribal commerce and to provide jobs for tribal citizens. Prior to formation of tribal corporations, employment opportunities in tribal communities had been limited to employment within the tribal social and governmental services programs, the facilities and maintenance operations for tribal buildings, elected positions within tribal government, and employment with local non-tribal businesses. With the entry of tribal corporations, employment opportunities for tribal citizens substantially increased in addition to opportunities for non-tribal citizens in local communities.

Thus, tribal corporations serve as engines of commercial growth in economically-depressed communities with the profits returning to tribal government to support the tribal and local community. Likewise, ANCs are regarded as the economic structures to provide sustainable economic development for many rural Alaska Native communities. Native Hawaiian Organizations (NHOs) are intended to support community development as well for their membership.

A further avenue for strengthening the profitability of tribal corporations, ANCs and NHOs occurred with their inclusion in the Small Business Administration's 8(a) federal contracting program for small and disadvantaged businesses. Within the federal law authorizing government contracts for socially and economically disadvantaged businesses, an express provision for economically disadvantaged Indian tribes was built-in at section 15 U.S.C. §637(a)(4) in 1986. The definition of "Indian tribes" is provided at 15 U.S.C. §637(a)(9)(F)(13) to include "any Indian tribe, band, nation or other organized group or community of Indians, including any Alaska Native village or regional or village corporation (within the meaning of the Alaska Native Claims Settlement Act)" and has recognition as such by the federal government or a state government. Further, Native Hawaiian Organizations are also eligible for the 8(a) Program as defined at 15 U.S.C. §637(a)(9)(F)(15).

The Native 8(a) Program is structured as a nine-year program that allows economically disadvantaged tribally-owned businesses, Alaska Native corporations (ANCs), and NHOs to receive preference when bidding on government contracts, 13 C.F.R. §124.2. These business entities have exemptions provided for in the Native 8(a) Program that allow for non-capped sole source government contract awards and allow multiple subsidiaries to apply for separate bidding opportunities, 13 C.F.R. §124.519. The availability of such sole source awards was severely limited, however, following a new provision enacted as part of the National Defense Authorization Act for Fiscal Year 2010 (P.L. 111-84).

The new provision has been incorporated as of March 16, 2011 into the Code of Federal Regulations at 48 C.F.R. §6.303-2(d) and provides that any federal agency prior to awarding a sole source contract under the 8(a) Program for an amount over $20 million must issue a Justification & Approval (J&A). The J&A must be approved in writing by a high level federal procurement officer as set forth in 48 C.F.R. §6.304. Further, the J&A must be provided publicly, 48 C.F.R. §6.305. By requiring federal procurement officers to comply with more onerous processes, it is anticipated that this new requirement will deter the awarding of the sole-source contracts previously only available to tribal corporations, ANCs and NHOs. The new provision grew out of recent negative congressional and media attention on the Native 8(a) Program which was viewed as unjustified by the Native American Contractors Association since Native 8(a) contracts compose less than 1% of the annual federal contracts awarded on an annual basis.

The intention for allowing the Native 8(a) exemptions was to provide economic incentives to grow tribal businesses in some of the most impoverished regions in the U.S. As stated previously, tribally-owned corporations, ANCs, and NHOs provide benefits for entire communities unlike other for-profit enterprises individually-owned. The Native Hawaiian Organizations Association emphasizes that profits derived by NHOs are used to support "youth programs, access to legal defense, leadership development, innovative youth education, specialized job training, health, financial literacy, business development, cultural engagement, community development, and other community needs," according to its website.

On the national level, the Native American Contractors Association (NACA) serves as a consortium for the Native 8(a) Program and actively monitors developments in federal business policy impacting the program. This serves as an example of Tribal Nations continuing to organize as confederacies advancing mutual economic interests in contemporary times.

d. The Tribal Gaming and Tourist Industries

Historically, Native Americans engaged in social gambling activities and later were encouraged to play bingo as a pastime after church services by reservation missionaries. From these activities, tribal governments developed commercial bingo halls and invited consumers from on- and off-reservation to participate. The first such commercial bingo operation has been attributed to the Seminole Tribe of Florida opening its enterprise in 1979. In the mid-1980s, state officials sought to close down tribal bingo operations that provided higher bet limits or jackpots than the state-regulated gaming operations. In Florida and California, litigation ensued that would eventually lead to federal legislation regulating the operation of the tribal gaming industry.

The U.S. Supreme Court decision in *California v. Cabazon Band of Mission Indians*, 480 U.S. 202, 217–18 (1987), upheld inherent tribal authority to operate a commercial bingo hall by the Cabazon Band and found that the federal government had encouraged such economic development. In opposition attorneys for the state of California argued that pursuant to Public Law 280, California criminal laws applied when the tribal bingo hall operated outside the regulations of state and county gambling ordinances, 480 U.S. at 205. In the Court's decision a distinction was made between activities that were criminal/prohibitory where Public Law 208 jurisdiction was proper for the state and activities that were civil/regulatory which were exempt from the state's jurisdiction under Public Law 280, 480 U.S. at 208–211. Because California regulated bingo games and did not strictly prohibit gambling within the state, the Court held that Public Law 280 jurisdiction was not available to the state to regulate a tribal commercial activity on-reservation, 480 U.S. at 212.

Following the *Cabazon* decision in 1987, the U.S. Congress quickly responded with passage of new federal legislation, the Indian Gaming and Regulatory Act (IGRA) of 1988, 25 U.S.C. §2701, et seq. The IGRA provided a new federal regulatory framework for tribal gaming and established the National Indian Gaming Commission (NIGC) to implement the framework, 25 U.S.C. §2704-2708. The IGRA divided tribal gaming into three classes with different types of regulation required per class. Class I gaming was designated within the exclusive regulation of Tribal Nations, 25 U.S.C. §2710(a)(1), and includes the following types of gaming: "social games solely for prizes of minimal value or traditional forms of Indian gaming engaged in by individuals as a part of, or in connection with, tribal ceremonies or celebrations," 25 U.S.C. §2703(6).

For Class II gaming, the IGRA regulatory mechanisms are in full force through the NIGC and the requirements placed on tribal governments operating such gaming. The IGRA definitional section states that Class II gaming includes: all forms of electronic or manual bingo, certain types of card games which are authorized and not prohibited by state laws, and games not specifically excluded, 25 U.S.C. §2703(7)(A). The NIGC has published regulations defining the electronic games allowed under the Class II designation at 25 C.F.R. §502.7. Class II gaming excludes "any banking card games, including baccarat, chemin de fer, or blackjack (21)" or any slot machines, 25 U.S.C. §2703(7)(B).

The basic requirements a tribal government must meet to operate Class II gaming on tribal lands include the requirement that the surrounding state does not prohibit gambling, the NIGC has approved the tribal laws governing the operation of Class II tribal gaming, and gaming revenues must be spent in the five ways authorized by the IGRA as demonstrated in an annual audit submitted to the NIGC for review, 25 U.S.C. §2710. Furthermore, the tribal government must contribute a percentage of its proceeds from Class II gaming to the operating budget of the National Indian Gaming Commission, 25 U.S.C.§2717.

Under the IGRA, tribal governments can expend net revenues from Class II gaming enterprises for five purposes or be in violation of the federal law. The five authorized use of these tribal revenues are: 1) "to fund tribal government operations or programs;" 2) "to provide for the general welfare of the Indian tribe and its members;" 3) "to promote tribal economic development;" 4) "to donate to charitable organizations;" or 5) "to help fund operations of local governments," 25 U.S.C. § 2710(b)(2)(B). Tribal gaming businesses are the only types of non-federally-operated businesses in the United States that are directed to expend their revenues as dictated by federal statute.

In the IGRA, Class III gaming includes any other type of gaming not included in Class I and Class II, or simply all types of casino games, 25 U.S.C. § 2703(8). For a tribal government to operate a Class III gaming facility, the following requirements must be met: approval of a tribal gaming ordinance by the NIGC, the surrounding state must authorize some form of gaming within its borders, and a compact between the Tribe and the surrounding state must be approved by the Secretary of the Interior, 25 U.S.C. § 2710(d).

The Tribal-State compacting process has given rise to litigation in federal courts resulting in a key provision being stricken from the IGRA. In the original text of the IGRA, Tribes were directed to file suit in federal court when a state authorizing gaming refused to negotiate in good faith with the Tribe to enter into a Tribal-State compact. In 1996, the U.S. Supreme Court held in *Seminole Tribe of Florida v. Florida,* 517 U.S. 44, 72–73, that the U.S. Congress lacked the authority to legislate within the IGRA a waiver of state sovereign immunity. Thus, the remedy for Tribes to file suit in federal court when states failed to negotiate in good faith was only available if the state government agreed to waive the sovereign immunity embodied in the U.S. Constitution's Eleventh Amendment.

Tribes continue to negotiate for Class III gaming with surrounding states to operate gaming facilities on tribal lands. When negotiations are entered into for a Tribal-State gaming compact, the IGRA provides the subjects of such negotiations, 25 U.S.C. § 2710(d)(3)(C). Many states entering into Tribal-State compacts have sought payments from the Tribes labeled as "revenue sharing" provisions. The IGRA expressly forbids states to impose taxes through the compacting process, but payments in lieu of taxes and revenue sharing for exclusivity in operating regions have been approved by the Secretary of the Interior. Under the IGRA, the Secretary of the Interior must approve the compact prior to the tribal government commencing Class III gaming.

As early as 1985, Tribal Nations organized a national association to further tribal economic initiatives in the gaming industry. The National Indian Gaming Association (NIGA) currently has 184 tribal government members. One of the stated purposes of NIGA is "to maintain and protect Indian sovereign governmental authority in Indian Country" according to the Association's web site. NIGA reported in the 2009 "Economic Impact of Indian Gaming" report that 237 Tribal Nations in 28 states generated $26.2 billion gross income from gaming enterprises. Gaming enterprises in Indian Country also serve the function of providing employment opportunities in tribal communities. From this same report, an estimated 628,000 jobs were provided by tribal governmental gaming operations in 2009.

The tribal gaming industry has provided tribal governments across the country with an opportunity to provide employment opportunities, accumulate capital to diversify into other industries and build commercial relationships in contemporary markets. A small percentage of tribal governments have experienced huge financial gains by locating gaming operations in close proximity to large urban areas.

As Tribal Nations have gained expertise in the gaming industry, many have expanded into adding resort features to the gaming facility. Tourism has become increasingly important to tribal economies and attracting tourists on vacation or for events to tribal entertainment centers has developed over the last decade. Additions to the original casino may include a five star hotel, on-site spa, golf course, a variety of dining options, entertainment facilities for concerts, indoor water parks, and play centers for children. Tribal resorts have full-scale marketing for featured events, such as headliner bands, boxing matches and national poker tournaments. This area of tribal economic development will likely continue to expand in the coming decades as Tribal Nations highlight tribal cultural museums and shopping unique to their people and provide one-of-a-kind experiences for tourists.

C. Tribal Business Laws, Employment and Taxation

Tribal laws provide for taxation of businesses operating within the tribal territory. Tribal government legislates on the amount of tax to be assessed, the requirements for business licenses and for vendors entering the tribal domain. Best practices for opening a business in Indian Country begins with contacting the tribal tax office for information on the current rate schedule for business taxes, on registering to do business in the tribal jurisdiction, on obtaining a business license, and on complying with tribal laws. Tribal governments often have delegated authority to a planning or land use department to provide recommendations on tribal zoning ordinances to provide for effective management of economic development on tribal lands. Businesses seeking to locate in Indian Country should consult such tribal departments to adequately comply with the community layout on tribal lands.

1. Employment Preference for Tribal Members

Tribal governments have followed the U.S. government in creating Indian preference statutes to provide priority in the hiring of tribal members for businesses operating in the tribal territory. The U.S. government, in the Indian Reorganization Act of 1934, legislated a preference for Indian people to be employed in federal positions related to Indian affairs, 25 U.S.C. §472. In 1974, the U.S. Supreme Court held in *Morton v. Mancari*, 417 U.S. 535, 554–555, that the federal Indian preference was based on the Tribal-U.S. political relationship and did not constitute invidious racial discrimination towards non-Indians employed in the Bureau of Indian Affairs. Rather, the Court focused on the goal of furthering Indian self-government by employing American Indians in federal Indian programs as the proper purpose of the statute, 417 U.S. at 554.

Similarly, tribal governments have enacted employment preferences for tribal members in the first instance. Private businesses operating within the tribal jurisdiction and contracting with the tribal government will be expected to follow the tribal preference statutes. Often, tribal governments will require specific language in business contracts implementing tribal preference in hiring for construction projects or other business ventures on tribal lands. The governmental office monitoring the preference statute is commonly referred to as the Tribal Employment Rights Office or "TERO." The goal of tribal employment preferences is to provide opportunities for tribal members to have jobs within their home communities, particularly when the tribal government is engaged in economic activity.

2. Taxation in the Tribal Jurisdiction

Tribal laws establish sales taxes on motor fuels, cigarette purchases, leases, and other transactions in a blanket fashion for all who engage in tribal commerce. Federal taxation applies to individual income of tribal members, tribal employment activities, and tribal gaming per capita payments under the IGRA, 25 U.S.C. §2710(b)(3)(D). Tribal member income derived from an allotment is exempt from federal taxation as are payments under treaties, federal settlement acts or other federal laws, I.R.S. Revenue Ruling 67-284. Tribal government corporations are not subject to a federal corporate tax, I.R.S. Revenue Ruling 94-16.

In a series of U.S. Supreme Court decisions, the Court has determined that states have concurrent taxing authority for commercial activity of non-members doing business in the tribal jurisdiction. The U.S. Supreme Court has upheld the general principle that state governments cannot directly tax tribal governments or tribal members within tribal lands. In the 1976 decision of *Moe v. Confederated Salish and Kootenai Tribes of the Flathead Reservation*, 425 U.S. 463, the Court held that the state of Montana could not impose taxes on tribal lands for cigarette sales to tribal members, a license fee for tribal vendors selling cigarettes or for property taxes on vehicles located on tribal lands, 425 U.S. at 480–481. As for Montana's imposition of a cigarette sales tax on purchases by non-members at tribal smoke shops located on tribal lands, the Court stated "[t]he State requirement that the Indian tribal seller collect a tax validly imposed on non-Indians is a minimal burden designed to avoid the likelihood that in its absence non-Indians purchasing from the tribal seller will avoid payment of a concededly lawful tax," 425 U.S. at 483. Thus, state governments have asserted a right to tax non-tribal members when they enter reservation boundaries and the U.S. Supreme Court has upheld such taxes.

With the U.S. Supreme Court sanctioning state taxation on purchases by non-tribal members, tribal government must weigh the decision to add tribal taxes to these same purchases. Double taxation of a good available off-reservation subject to only single taxation discourages consumers from making purchases on-reservation. In the interest of offering goods at competitive rates, the tribal government may choose to not impose a tribal tax alongside the state tax for non-member purchases. The negative consequence for tribal government is loss of tax revenue to support basic governmental services, such as road maintenance, social service programs, and support for education on tribal lands.

Collection of state taxes imposed within tribal lands has been an area of friction in the last several decades. The U.S. Supreme Court has provided guidance to state governments by upholding pre-collection of taxes prior to taxable goods entering tribal lands and by upholding imposition of state taxes in the chain of distribution before reaching the tribal lands. In *Wagnon v. Prairie Band of Potawatomi*, 546 U.S. 95 (2003), the U.S. Supreme Court approved a Kansas tax law imposing a motor fuels tax on the fuel distributor where the fuel was purchased by the Potawatomi Tribe at a purchase price that included the state tax. The Court stated that the legal incidence of the tax fell on the non-Indian distributor and thus, was not a direct tax on the tribal fuel station, 546 U.S. at 106–108. This area of regulatory jurisdiction through governmental taxing authority requires a careful and thorough analysis for any business operating in tribal territories.

TAXATION WITHIN TRIBAL COMMUNITIES:
BEST PRACTICE ANALYSIS

Step One — Tribal Government has inherent authority to tax within the tribal territorial boundaries.

Taxes are administered through a Tribal Tax Code and implemented through a Tribal Department of Revenue/Tax.

Step Two — Review Federal Statutes Imposing Federal and State taxation within the Tribal Jurisdiction:

Possible sources of federal taxes: Internal Revenue Code, Federal statutes on Oil, Gas, or Mineral Production on Tribal Lands
Possible sources of state taxes: State Taxation Code, Tribal-State Gaming Compact for Class III gaming, Tribal-State Tax Agreements

Step Three — Review U.S. Supreme Court Decisions Holding State Concurrent Taxation for Sales/Leases/Transactions for Non-Tribal Members:

States share concurrent taxation authority within tribal territorial boundaries for state taxes imposed upon sales/leases/transactions for non-members.

Step Four — Determine all sources of tax applicable to activity conducted on tribal lands.

Agreements between tribal governments and state governments on taxation will be further discussed in Chapter 8: "Tribal-State Relations."

D. Best Practices for Business Certainty in Tribal Communities

In general, business flourishes where certainty exists. For tribal governments, best practices to encourage and support business on tribal land include: providing clear tribal laws and regulations available publicly for potential investors and business owners; providing limited waivers of sovereign immunity for fair dealings in contracting; maintaining a strong tribal court system to handle disputes and provide fair resolutions; and engaging in zoning for industry, residential, retail, tribal governmental development, and economic conservation areas.

For state incorporated businesses seeking to do business in tribal lands, best practices include becoming versed in tribal laws on taxation, licensing and employment preferences; understanding the tribal goal of providing employment opportunities for tribal members; and familiarization with the tribal court system for dispute resolution. One of the significant benefits of doing business in Indian Country is the ability to partner with and contribute to an entire community.

There is also a growing trend in Indian Country for tribal businesses to seek contracting opportunities with other tribal businesses. With tribal-government owned businesses serving as the economic engine in tribal communities, private tribal member businesses are seeking ways in which to provide services to the larger tribal corporations and industries. In pursuing these tribal economic networks, the tribal trade route model is being re-energized across North America.

Checkpoints

- Tribal nations have engaged in trading partnerships and alliances with Europeans prior to the formation of the United States. With the limitations imposed by federal law on tribal resources and governance, tribal governments have prioritized economic development.

- Tribally-owned corporations may be established pursuant to a tribal constitution, through approval of a federal charter or under state law. Tribal government officials determine the structure of the corporate leadership.

- Federal programs, such as Native 8(a), provide incentives to tribally-owned corporations to participate in the federal procurement process and federally designated economically depressed areas.

- The tribal gaming industry operates pursuant to the Indian Gaming Regulatory Act (IGRA) containing many specific requirements that tribal government licensed gaming facilities must comply with. The National Indian Gaming Commission is the direct federal agency that implements the provisions of the IGRA.

- Tribal entities have sovereign immunity from lawsuits unless expressly waived in a contract. Best commercial practices are to waive sovereign immunity up to the amount of a contract; designate a specific court and body of law to resolve disputes in the contract; and act with good faith in all commercial dealings.

- Taxation is a key component to supporting tribal governmental services. Tribal tax offices and agencies operate under tribal law overseeing issuance of business licenses, employment preferences, and calculation of tribal taxes.

Chapter 6

Family Law in Tribal Communities

Roadmap

- Learn about the historical tribal restorative justice principles that applied to resolving issues involving family interactions.

- Learn about the impacts of early U.S. Indian policy intended to assimilate American Indian families into a model of Euro-Christian farmers. The assimilation practices implemented during this time period continue to affect tribal families.

- Understand the development of Tribal Courts as upholding tribal family values in dispute resolution and family law issues.

- Understand the history leading to the enactment of the federal Indian Child Welfare Act and its continued importance in tribal communities.

At the heart of every society are the principles that define and shape family life. For tribal peoples, traditionally the domestic sphere of life was in harmony with the governance structure of clans and the roles of each family member. The immediate and extended family formed a circle of relations around each person born or adopted into the Tribe. In Native languages, relative terms were employed to identify the speaker and the listener, underscoring a kinship relationship.

A. Principles of Restorative Justice in Historical Family Law Situations

Historically, family life in tribal communities naturally included common human disagreements and disruptions followed by efforts at reconciliation and resolution. Certain clans could be designated to provide mediators for disputes or certain wise individuals. Disruption to the social fabric was viewed as requiring a realignment of relationships to bring the society back into balance. Restorative justice principles allowed for families to engage in the resolution process and require actions of the individuals in disharmony to make amends. A common way to conclude a restorative justice event was to provide a feast and dance for the entire community to demonstrate the return to harmony.

Family law as it is understood in contemporary times involves children, juveniles, elders, marriages, and domestic relations. These groups and issues are integral to the expression of values and social norms within tribal communities. From the historical practices of family life to the contemporary, the ability of tribal communities to positively impact family law has been shaken by U.S. Indian laws and policies. In this chapter, the impact of U.S. Indian policy on this aspect of tribal society will be examined in addition to the role of tribal judicial systems over the same time period to the present.

B. Impacts of Early U.S. Indian Policy Eras on Tribal Family Life

The devastation to tribal family life due to early U.S. Indian policies would be difficult to overstate. Inheriting the conflicts of the colonial governments, the newly formed U.S. engaged in warfare against tribal communities, leading to the killing of children, mothers, fathers, and families. When the U.S. Indian policy changed to one of removal and reservation containment, tribal family members died in the hundreds during forced marches, through severe hot weather conditions for some and brutal cold for others, across great expanses of country. The removal policy was intended to open up land areas for the benefit of white land speculators and to encourage white settlement. Once on reservation areas, starvation often set in as hunting, fishing and territorial harvesting were forbidden by U.S. Indian agents. Disease, famine, and warfare were the primary features of U.S. Indian policy for most tribal communities, leading to long term social disruption, deep mourning periods, depression, post-traumatic stress, and a legacy of suicide.

After the removal and reservation eras, U.S. Indian policy switched to assimilation and allotment. A major thrust of the assimilation policy was aimed directly at tribal children. Throughout the late 1800s and up through the mid-1900s, the U.S. Indian policy on education was to remove children from tribal communities and send them to distant boarding schools to receive educational, vocational, and "civilization" training. The trauma experienced by the tribal community in having their children taken and the trauma experienced by the children, some as young as young as 4 years old, to be taken to a foreign military-style boarding school environment was intense and long lasting. The Bureau of Indian Affairs provided federal funding, often from treaty payments due to Tribes, for either the direct administration of federal boarding schools or to support Christian religious organizations administering boarding schools.

In 1928, the government authorized a survey on U.S. Indian policy impacts, "The Problem of Indian Administration," commonly known as the "Meriam Report" after the principal author, Lewis Meriam. The Meriam Report reviewed Indian education policy and the conditions at the boarding schools and strongly condemned both under the Indian Service Administration. For example, the low salaries and qualifications of key personnel in the government-run boarding schools were highlighted as follows.

> *Matrons and "Disciplinarians."* One of the best illustrations of the need for better equipped personnel is in the case of such positions as "matron" and "disciplinarian." The very words reflect an erroneous conception of the task that needs to be done; but whatever they are called, the positions need to be filled by people with appropriate training for this work. The matron of an Indian school influences the lives of boys and girls probably more than any other person on the staff. Education is essentially changing human behavior, for good or ill, and the manner in which the matron and disciplinarian handle the children in their care determines very largely the habits and attitudes that will go to make up what the outside world regards as their personality and character.
>
> It seems almost incredible that for a position as matron the educational requirement is only eighth grade — and even this eighth grade standard is comparatively new. (Meriam Report, Chapter 6, 1928).

The disciplinarian nature of these mandatory educational institutions, the long distances from tribal families, and the abuse that was experienced by the children have left lasting impacts on American Indian communities to this day.

Further, the manner of operating the government-run boarding schools added an additional burden on the children forced to attend. The system was set up as a half-day plan with the children serving as the laborers in every capacity for the other half of the day. The Meriam Report took issue with this entrenched practice.

> At present the half-day plan is felt to be necessary, not because it can be defended on health or educational grounds, for it cannot, but be-

cause the small amount of money allowed for food and clothes makes it necessary to use child labor. The official Course of Study for Indian Schools says frankly:

> In our Indian schools a large amount of productive work is nec-
> essary. They could not possibly be maintained on the amounts
> appropriated by Congress for their support were it not for the fact
> that students [*i.e.*, children] are required to do the washing, iron-
> ing, baking, cooking, sewing; to care for the dairy, farm, garden,
> grounds, buildings, etc.— an amount of labor that has in the ag-
> gregate a very appreciable monetary value. (Course of Study for
> United States Indian Schools, p. 1 (1922).

The term "child labor" is used advisedly. The labor of children as carried on in Indian boarding schools would, it is believed, constitute a
violation of child labor laws in most states. (Meriam Report, Chapter 6, 1928).

As several generations of American Indian children were mandated to the government and religious operated boarding schools, the cultural practices of
child-rearing, homemaking, plant stewardship, art techniques, tribal languages,
and hundreds of years of tribal knowledge were denied to these children as
they were brutally punished for exhibiting anything culturally tied to being an
American Indian. In the boarding schools and under the Indian agents on
reservations, Christianity was imposed as the only acceptable means of spiritual expression.

On the reservations, the Indian superintendent reigned with an iron fist.
Any parents refusing to allow their children to be taken to the boarding schools
would face any number of punishments by the Indian agent. Those labeled in-
surgents could face starvation as the Indian agents doled out basic subsistence
rations and would withhold rations as punishments. This was especially effective due to the labeling of any American Indians who ventured off the reservation as "hostiles" and subject to being shot by settlers or the U.S. military. Thus,
off-reservation hunting was not an option for most of the early and mid-1900s
following the establishment of the Indian reservations. The Courts of Indian
Offenses were also employed in meting out punishments against those who
resisted the U.S. government's assimilation policies.

C. Development and Role of Tribal Courts in Family Law

American Indians were not U.S. citizens unless a specific federal agreement or statute designated the citizenship status. In some treaties and allotment agreements, specific provisions set forth that by accepting an individual tract of land the Indian owner would become a dual citizen with both tribal citizenship and U.S. citizenship. By virtue of U.S. citizenship, tribal citizens would also legally become state citizens as well. The citizenship status of American Indians was important because state and federal courts barred those without U.S. citizenship from bringing cases. A famous example of the importance of American Indian classification under U.S. laws was the 1879 case, *Standing Bear v. Crooks* filed in the U.S. District Court in Omaha, Nebraska over which Judge Dundy presided. A family matter was at the core of the case.

Ponca leader, Standing Bear, had traveled from the Quapaw Reservation located in Indian Territory, present-day Oklahoma, back to his homelands to bury his deceased son in the lands that had become the state of Nebraska. The conditions of the Ponca Indians since removal from their homelands to Indian Territory had resulted in the deaths of almost one-third of the Tribe. In January of 1879, Standing Bear and a small group began the long arduous trek back to their homelands for the burial of his son, Bear Shield. They arrived at the Omaha Reservation in March of 1879 and were soon thereafter arrested and held at Fort Omaha under orders from General Crook. Local sympathy led to two attorneys advocating for Standing Bear and the Ponca group by filing a habeas corpus suit in federal court questioning the order of General Crooks to detain the group and return them to Indian Territory. A central issue to the case was whether Standing Bear was a person under U.S. law.

The attorney representing the U.S. government in the case, G.M. Lambertson, argued that Standing Bear as an American Indian did not exist legally as a person or as a citizen and could not bring suit against the United States government. Judge Dundy allowed Standing Bear to testify in the courtroom with the help of an interpreter. At the conclusion of the case, Judge Dundy issued his decision finding that an American Indian was a person under U.S. law; the habeas petition was properly brought before the court on behalf of Standing Bear; and that the Ponca group had the right to return and remain in their homelands. As a result, Standing Bear and the other tribal members were set free from U.S. military custody and carried forward the burial of Bear Shield on the banks of the Niobrara River. This case serves as an example of the legal standing of American Indians prior to the passage of the 1924 Indian Citizenship Act, 43 Stat. 253 Act of June 2, 1924, and demonstrates the lengths tribal peoples have went to in order to properly carry out family obligations.

With the assimilation policies of the late 1800s outlawing Indian practices, forums to resolve disputes through traditional cultural ways were no longer available to most tribal communities. As discussed in Chapter 3 following the U.S. Supreme Court ruling in *Ex Parte Crow Dog*, 109 U.S. 556 (1883), that the federal courts lacked criminal jurisdiction for tribal member against tribal member crime in Indian Country, the U.S. Congress enacted the Major Crimes Act of 1885, 18 U.S.C. § 1153, asserting federal jurisdiction over crimes where the alleged perpetrator was American Indian and the crime was specifically listed in the Act. See Chapter 3 Criminal Jurisdiction in Indian Country on how federal criminal jurisdiction has since been expanded on tribal lands. Also in 1883, the U.S. Indian Service began setting up Courts of Indian Offenses handling both criminal and civil matters on Indian reservations.

The Code of Indian Offenses enforced by these courts outlawed cultural practices and served as a tool of assimilation for the local Indian agent. To foster the legitimacy of these early courts in Indian Country, tribal people were commonly selected by the Indian agent to serve as tribal judges. As U.S. Indian policy shifted to recognition of tribal constitutional forms of government, tribal courts were formalized in the constitutions. Tribes that did not adopt tribal constitutions also set up tribal court systems during this time period, such as the Navajo Nation.

Many tribal constitutions allow for the appointment and removal of judges to be vested in the tribal council. Thus, tribal councils may have the authority to remove a tribal judge in the aftermath of an unpopular court decision. Some tribal constitutions have been amended or contained provisions allowing for the initial appointment of a tribal judge by the tribal council and then subsequent elections to renew employment for the judge. Tribal governments have the ability to choose the process of appointing and/or electing judges to fit the particular needs of the tribal court. The judicial system is a key component to every modern government and should be insulated from pressure by political bodies to assure parties before the court that they will receive a fair hearing and just resolution.

Best practices for tribal judge positions may include the establishment of either a tribal court administrator or a tribal judiciary board to vet candidates and then submit recommendations for appointment to the tribal council. The election process for tribal judges may be another best practice that ensures community engagement in the selection of decision-makers for the tribal court system. Above all the tribal judge position should not be vulnerable to political removal or to influence in the decision-making role of the judge. For the Navajo Nation judicial system, a candidate for a judgeship must be approved by the

Navajo Nation President and the Navajo Council to serve a two-year probationary period. Once that period is satisfactorily completed, then the judge is sent through the approval process once more and if approved has a lifetime appointment in the Navajo Nation judicial system. An online resource on Tribal Court formation, structure, and operation is the Tribal Court Clearinghouse project of the Tribal Law and Policy Institute at: http://www.tribal-institute.org/lists/codes.htm.

One of the primary functions of a tribal court is to provide a forum for resolution of family law matters and issues arising from the domestic sphere of tribal life. The formalities involved in marriage, divorce, child custody, child support, familial visitation, adoptions, establishing paternity, and other matters concerning the family are all within the purview of the tribal court. Tribal courts are ideally suited for resolving family law issues as institutions that are tied to the local community, society and norms. Tribal courts apply tribal law and tribal values to resolve disputes, to manage family relations as necessary, to handle the disposition of estates and to distribute property in probate matters. One of the continued barriers to full tribal autonomy lies in the probate arena, where the United States as the legal title holder to Indian lands continues to exert jurisdiction over real property matters at death. As such, tribal courts may hear personal property matters and other end of life issues, but may have to wait for years of federal backlog to have closure on the full range of probate matters.

D. Tribal Children and Contemporary Laws

Tribal children are the ones who will carry forward the tribal culture, the tribal lifeways, the tribal government, and the tribal existence. Tribal Nations depend on tribal children to ensure that the tribal community continues on into the future. Throughout the history of the relationship with the United States, tribal children have been especially vulnerable to the assimilation policies of federal officials. After the devastating impacts of the mandatory government boarding school policies up to the early 1950s, tribal children were once again targeted for incorporation into white mainstream society through the process of state court adoptions.

1. The Systematic Adoption of Indian Children in the 1950s–1970s

Beginning in the late 1950s through the 1970s, American Indian children were removed from their home tribal communities through a concerted effort of federal, state and private agencies. One such program was the federally-supported Indian Adoption Project. From approximately 1958–1967, the Bureau of Indian Affairs and the U.S. Children's Bureau federally-funded the Indian Adoption Project which was implemented by the Child Welfare League of America. The Project specifically sought out children with one-fourth degree or more American Indian blood on western reservations and placed them in white homes in midwestern and eastern states. Officially, 395 American Indian children were adopted into white families across the United States through the Indian Adoption Project's efforts. This official Project number doesn't represent the full picture of the push for Indian children adoptions. In the report of March 15, 1966 by Project Director Arnold Lyslo, survey results indicated that 696 Indian children had been "adopted out" of tribal communities in the year 1965 alone by over 90 agencies operating in states with large American Indian populations. This removal of American Indian children from tribal communities occurred during the Termination Era of U.S. Indian policy and worked to diminish the number of tribal members under the responsibility of the BIA.

State social workers also played a role in the removal of children from tribal homes during this time period. Using ambiguous characterizations of "neglect" for American Indian children in Indian homes, state and county social workers placed the children into mostly non-Indian foster care homes and eventually into adoptive placements. The Association on American Indians prepared a report for the U.S. Congress in the 1970s finding that from 25–35% of all American Indian children were in placements outside of their homes. Across the country, tribal leaders and organizations began a five-year lobbying effort for federal legislation to address the removal of Indian children from their tribal homes.

2. The Provisions of the Indian Child Welfare Act of 1978

As a result, the Indian Child Welfare Act, 25 U.S.C. § 1901 et seq. was passed in 1978. In the first section of the federal law, the congressional findings included the following:

> (3) that there is no resource that is more vital to the continued existence and integrity of Indian tribes than their children and that the United States has a direct interest, as trustee, in protecting Indian children who are members of or are eligible for membership in an Indian tribe;
> (4) that an alarmingly high percentage of Indian families are broken up by the removal, often unwarranted, of their children from

them by nontribal public and private agencies and that an alarmingly high percentage of such children are placed in non-Indian foster and adoptive homes and institutions; and

(5) that the States, exercising their recognized jurisdiction over Indian child custody proceedings through administrative and judicial bodies, have often failed to recognize the essential tribal relations of Indian people and the cultural and social standards prevailing in Indian communities and families. 25 U.S.C. § 1901 (P.L. 95-608, § 2, Nov. 8, 1978, 92 Stat. 3069).

In addressing these alarming past practices by state social workers and state courts, the Indian Child Welfare Act (ICWA) operates as a jurisdictional transfer statute for cases involving the placement of Indian children outside of their parental homes. The ICWA provides that such cases are to be transferred from a state court to the appropriate tribal court, 25 U.S.C. § 1911(b). State court transfer of an Indian child placement case may be withheld upon a finding of "good cause to the contrary," an objection by either parent, or declination of the transfer by the tribal court, 25 U.S.C. § 1911(b). Another provision in the ICWA mandates that the child's Indian custodian or a tribal representative has the right to intervene in any state court proceeding involving the placement of the Indian child, 25 U.S.C. § 1911(c).

3. Preliminary Core Principles for the Application of the Indian Child Welfare Act

Two preliminary core principles are important in understanding the operation of the ICWA. First is the definition of Indian child for the law to apply and second is the type of court proceedings where the ICWA becomes operative. The ICWA states the definition of Indian child as follows: " 'Indian child' means any unmarried person who is under age eighteen and is either (a) a member of an Indian tribe or (b) is eligible for membership in an Indian tribe and is the biological child of a member of an Indian tribe," 25 U.S.C. § 1903(4). Thus, the membership criteria set in each Tribe's laws are of great significance in determining whether the ICWA will apply to a child in a state court placement proceeding. As discussed in the Introduction to this book, tribal membership has been tied to blood quantum standards set by the federal government and such standards are often entrenched in the contemporary tribal constitutions developed by the BIA in the 1930s.

The second preliminary core principle for application of the ICWA is the type of state court proceeding which will involve this federal law. The ICWA applies to an Indian child subject to a child custody proceeding in state court. As provided in the definition section of the ICWA, a child custody proceeding includes the following: foster care placement, termination of parental rights, preadoptive placement, and adoptive placement, 25 U.S.C. § 1903(1)(i)-(iv). In short, any placement of an Indian child outside of the parental home or the legal guardian home would involve application of the ICWA. Therefore, the ICWA is not operative for divorce proceedings where a child is placed in the custody of one parent or where joint custody is granted to both parents.

4. Exclusive Tribal Jurisdiction and Domicile

Within the ICWA, tribal court jurisdiction is recognized as exclusive for child placement proceedings where either: 1) the Indian child is the ward of the tribal court or 2) the Indian child is a resident or domiciled within the reservation of the child's tribe, 25 U.S.C. § 1911(a). The federal law does not define "resident" or "domicile" in the definitions section, 25 U.S.C. § 1903.

In 1989, the United States Supreme Court in *Mississippi Band of Choctaw v. Holyfield,* 490 U.S. 30, addressed the definition of "domicile" to determine whether the Mississippi Choctaw Tribal Court had exclusive jurisdiction over a voluntary adoption proceeding for twin babies. The case involved unwed parents both of whom were enrolled in the Mississippi Choctaw Tribe, lived on the Mississippi Choctaw reservation, and both of whom signed a consent-to-adoption form for the twins, 490 U.S. at 37–38. The local county court near the hospital where the mother gave birth entered the decree of adoption and did not refer to the Indian Child Welfare Act in the proceeding. Two months after the decree was entered in the county court the Tribe filed a motion to vacate the decree on the ground that exclusive jurisdiction over the infants was in the tribal court. The county court overruled the motion relying on the fact that the mother was off-reservation when the children were born and therefore, the children had never resided on the reservation, 490 U.S. at 38–39. On appeal, the Supreme Court of Mississippi affirmed and stated that the Tribe's argument was creative in asserting that the babies in their mother's womb lived on the reservation. In doing so, the court did not follow state court cases holding that a child's domicile followed that of the child's parents, 490 U.S. at 40.

In the U.S. Supreme Court, the court held that the state courts had failed to correctly apply the ICWA along with the common law principle that children are domiciled where their parents were domiciled. Under the ICWA, the decision stated that the situation was clearly governed by that federal law as the state court proceeding was within the definition of a "child custody proceeding" and the twin babies were "Indian children," 490 U.S. at 42.

Turning to the definition of the word "domicile" as critical to the operation of the federal law, the Court held that Congress did not intend for each state to define the term and give uneven results to the Indian Child Welfare Act. In fact, the Court's opinion pointed out that "the congressional findings that are a part of the statute demonstrate that Congress perceived the States and their courts as partly responsible for the problem it intended to correct," 490 U.S. at 45. In applying the generally accepted definition of a minor's domicile, the Court's opinion stated the following.

> It is undisputed in this case that the domicile of the mother (as well as the father) has been, at all relevant times, on the Choctaw Reservation. Tr. of Oral Arg. 28–29. Thus, it is clear that at their birth the twin babies were also domiciled on the reservation, even though they themselves had never been there. The statement of the Supreme Court of Mississippi that "[a]t no point in time can it be said the twins ... were domiciled within the territory set aside for the reservation," 511 So.2d, at 921, may be a correct statement of that State's law of domicile, but it is inconsistent with generally accepted doctrine in this country and cannot be what Congress had in mind when it used the term in the ICWA. 490 U.S. at 48–49.

Noting that parents cannot defeat the provisions of the ICWA and cut the children's ties with the Tribe and that three years in litigation may have led to bonding with the adoptive parents, the U.S. Supreme Court concluded by upholding the language of the ICWA and finding exclusive jurisdiction in the tribal court, 490 U.S. at 52–55. In exercising its exclusive jurisdiction, the Mississippi Choctaw Tribal Court then approved the adoption to the non-Indians parents and required the adoptive parents to maintain contact with the children's tribal relatives.

5. The ICWA Procedural Safeguards for Involuntary Proceedings in State Courts

If the child custody proceeding does occur in state court, then the ICWA mandates procedural standards to uphold the purposes of the law. The state court is first mandated to send notice by registered mail to the child's Tribe and parent/custodian of any pending proceeding involving the Indian child and of the right of intervention in that proceeding, 25 U.S.C. § 1912(a). The court may not proceed with a placement or a termination of parental rights until at least ten days after the child's Tribe and parent/custodian have received the notice.

25 U.S.C. § 1912(a). Further, after notice is received, an additional twenty days to prepare may be requested by the child's Tribe and/or parent/custodian, 25 U.S.C. § 1912(a). The parent or Indian custodian of the child may be appointed an attorney for any removal, placement or termination of rights proceeding upon a determination of indigency or financial need by the court, 25 U.S.C. § 1912(b). Finally, the court may appoint an attorney to represent the Indian child when it would be "in the best interest of the child" in any removal, placement or termination of parental rights proceeding, 25 U.S.C. § 1912(b).

On June 25, 2013, the United States Supreme Court handed down its second opinion involving interpretation of the provisions of the Indian Child Welfare Act, *Adoptive Couple v. Baby Girl*, 570 U.S. ___ (2013). The 5-4 decision held that an Indian biological father who did not have physical or legal custody of his daughter was not covered under the protections of § 1912(f). In that case, a Cherokee father sought to intervene in South Carolina state court proceedings where the non-Indian unwed birth mother voluntarily placed their daughter born in Oklahoma up for adoption. The majority concluded: "In sum, when, as here, the adoption of an Indian child is voluntarily and lawfully initiated by a non-Indian parent with sole custodial rights, the ICWA's primary goal of preventing the unwarranted removal of Indian children and the dissolution of Indian families is not implicated," Slip Opinion at 10. The Court cited to the BIA Guidelines, 44 Fed. Reg. 67593 (1979) as supportive of this announced requirement of pre-existing custody by the Indian parent prior to application of the ICWA provisions for parental rights termination under § 1912(f) and the provisions for active efforts to rehabilitate the Indian family under § 1912(d). Further the opinion provided that no other alternative party sought adoption of the child and therefore the placement preferences in § 1915(a) did not need to be applied for the Indian child involved, Slip Opinion at 15. The case was ultimately remanded back to the highest court in South Carolina to determine proper custody of the Cherokee girl.

During the legal battle, the child had been returned to her Cherokee father in Oklahoma by order of the South Caroline Supreme Court. After the U.S. Supreme Court decision was announced, the father was scheduled to attend a 30 day out-of-state training as part of his U.S. military service. The Cherokee Nation District Court, following an emergency guardianship hearing ordered that the step-mother, and paternal grandparents, which included a Cherokee grandfather to serve as custodians of the child during the father's short military leave. Later the same day, the South Carolina Supreme Court remanded the adoption case back to a lower state court to finalize the adoption to the non-Indian couple and to terminate the Cherokee father's rights, as he was not entitled to the ICWA's parental rights termination protections. With the new situation that has arisen, more litigation will likely ensue. The litigation over the custody of this child as a citizen of the Cherokee Nation has involved the highest federal court in the United States, the highest state court in South Carolina, the courts of the state of Oklahoma and the District Court of the Cherokee Nation. This is an illustration of the complexity of jurisdiction involved due to the intersection of federal, state and tribal laws regarding tribal children.

Before a state court can order foster care placement of an Indian child or termination of parental rights, the state agency must prove to the court that a high level of efforts were made to support the Indian family and keep the family intact. The law expressly states that these efforts must be "active efforts" demonstrating that the Indian family received "remedial services and rehabilitative programs designed to prevent the breakup of the Indian family and that these efforts have proved unsuccessful," 25 U.S.C. §1912(d). For an Indian child to be placed in foster care, the court must determine by the high standard of "clear and convincing evidence" that the placement is necessary to prevent "serious emotional or physical damage" to the Indian child, 25 U.S.C. §1912(e). When the state court must determine whether parental rights should be terminated, the ICWA asserts a very high standard for such a determination. The state court can only terminate parental rights if there is sufficient evidence to establish beyond a reasonable doubt "that the continued custody of the child by the parent or Indian custodian is likely to result in serious emotional or physical damage to the child," 25 U.S.C. §1912(f).

If the state court determines that the Indian child will be placed in foster care, then the ICWA has established placement preferences that are mandatory unless good cause to the contrary is found, 25 U.S.C. §1915(b). The order for placement of an Indian child in foster care is as follows:

> (i) a member of the Indian child's extended family;
> (ii) a foster home licensed, approved, or specified by the Indian child's tribe;
> (iii) an Indian foster home licensed or approved by an authorized non-Indian licensing authority; or
> (iv) an institution for children approved by an Indian tribe or operated by an Indian organization which has a program suitable to meet the Indian child's needs.

The court is directed to follow a tribal resolution of the child's Tribe if a different preference order has been designated, as long as the court finds the placement will be "the least restrictive setting appropriate" for the particular child's needs, 25 U.S.C. §1915(c). For the adoption of an Indian child under state law, the preference for the adoptive home is: "(1) a member of the child's extended family; (2) other members of the Indian child's tribe; or (3) other Indian families" unless there is good cause to the contrary for following this order of preference, 25 U.S.C. § 1915(a). These same placement preferences will apply to any Indian child's removal from one foster care placement to another type of placement whether another foster care placement, a preadoptive placement or an adoptive placement, 25 U.S.C. § 1916(b).

For both foster care and adoption placement, the court is directed to consider the cultural and social standards of the Indian child's tribal community in meeting the placement preference requirements. The ICWA identifies the appropriate community as "the Indian community in which the parent or extended family resides or with which the parent or extended family members maintain social and cultural ties," 25 U.S.C. § 1915(d). Also, the court shall ensure that the records of the foster care or adoptive placement are maintained by the state and available for review at any time upon the request of the child's Tribe or the Secretary of the Interior, 25 U.S.C. § 1915(e).

Within the federal law, the right to petition for the return of the Indian child that has been adopted is also provided for in certain situations. If an adoption decree is set aside or vacated for an Indian child, the Indian parent/custodian has the right to petition for the return of custody. Also if the adoptive parents voluntarily agree to terminate their parental rights to the Indian child, then the child's biological parent or the prior Indian custodian may file a petition requesting the return of the child, 25 U.S.C. § 1916(a). A court receiving the petition will grant such petition except when it would not be in the best interests of the child applying the evidentiary standards set forth in section 1912 of the ICWA, 25 U.S.C. § 1916(a).

6. Voluntary Foster Care Placement or Adoption of an Indian Child

The Indian Child Welfare Act also governs when the biological parent(s) of the Indian child voluntarily choose(s) to relinquish custody of the child either to foster care placement or the adoption process. This process was at issue in the prior discussion of the U.S. Supreme Court case, *Mississippi Band of Choctaw v. Holyfield*, 490 U.S. 30 (1989). The voluntariness of such an action must meet the strict requirements of the federal law. The consent to terminate parental rights must be in writing, given before a judge and the judge must file along with the consent a certificate verifying "that the terms and consequences of the consent were fully explained in detail and were fully understood by the parent or Indian custodian," 25 U.S.C. § 1913(a). No consent is valid within ten days prior to the birth of an Indian child or within the ten days following the birth, 25 U.S.C. § 1913(a).

As discussed above in *Adoptive Couple v. Baby Girl*, 570 U.S. ___ (2013), the U.S. Supreme Court's opinion indicated that when an Indian child has a non-

Indian parent with sole custody who enters into a voluntary adoption of the child then the ICWA provisions on termination of parental rights may not apply for the Indian parent. In other words, an Indian parent's rights are strongest when that parent has had custody of the Indian child. Each fact situation for a voluntary adoption of an Indian child must be carefully considered as a result of that U.S. Supreme Court opinion and the provisions of the ICWA.

When voluntary consent allows for placement of an Indian child in foster care, the parent or Indian custodian may withdraw his/her consent "at any time," 25 U.S.C. §1913(b). The Indian Child Welfare Act provides that once consent is withdrawn the child must be returned. In the situation of voluntary termination of parental rights, the parent may withdraw consent at any time up until the final decree of termination for any reason and the child shall be returned, 25 U.S.C. §1913(c). When an Indian child is voluntarily placed for adoption, the parent may again withdraw consent for any reason up until the final decree of adoption and the child shall be returned, 25 U.S.C. §1913(c). Further, the parent has the right to assert a challenge that his/her voluntary consent was obtained through fraud or duress within two years of an adoption decree. The parent may file a withdrawal of consent and petition the court to vacate the adoption decree for the return of the Indian child, 25 U.S.C. §1913(d). If state law provides for a longer time period than two years to assert a challenge, then that will be available to the parent, 25 U.S.C. §1913(d).

7. The Washington Indian Child Welfare Act and Tribal Court Exclusive Jurisdiction

The state of Washington's actions involving the federal Indian Child Welfare Act provide an example of the complexity and need for clarification that can arise in this area of family law. Under Public Law 280, the federal government delegated its criminal and limited civil forum access for certain matters arising in Indian Country to specific states; see Chapter Three for more information on this federal law. In the Washington state legislation accepting the federal Public Law 280 delegation, the state explicitly asserted jurisdiction over a number of areas involving American Indian children, including compulsory school attendance, domestic relations, adoption proceedings, and dependent children, RCW 37.12.010. State courts in Washington and elsewhere exercising such jurisdiction would still be subject to the case transfer provisions of the ICWA under 25 U.S.C. §1911(b) discussed previously. Further, the intervention rights in any state court child custody proceeding for the Indian parent/custodian and the child's Tribe would continue intact under 25 U.S.C. §1911(c). The interaction between the ICWA's designation of exclusive tribal jurisdiction and Washington Public Law 280 jurisdiction involving Indian children would be decisively clarified in state legislation in 2011.

The state of Washington provides an example of state proactive efforts through its Department of Social and Health Services (DSHS) to better implement the provisions and purpose of the ICWA. Following passage of the ICWA, the DSHS developed a manual on Indian Child Welfare policy for state caseworker practices and entered into specific tribal-state agreements on procedures. In 2004, tribal officials and DSHS officials held a summit to discuss solutions to the on-going problems and differing interpretations of the ICWA in state placement proceedings involving Indian children. From the summit, efforts turned to introducing state legislation incorporating the provisions of the ICWA and therefore, domesticating the federal law into state law. After almost seven years of revising draft legislation to meet concerns of legislators, adoption attorneys, foster care organizations, and tribal officials, the state law became effective July 22, 2011, RCW 13.38.010.

The relationships developed between the state DSHS and tribal officials provided the basis for incorporation of the ICWA into Washington state law and serves as a model for other state and tribal governments. By passing this state legislation, state legislators set forth the following intention.

> The legislature finds that the state is committed to protecting the essential tribal relations and best interests of Indian children by promoting practices designed to prevent out-of-home placement of Indian children that is inconsistent with the rights of the parents, the health, safety, or welfare of the children, or the interests of their tribe. Whenever out-of-home placement of an Indian child is necessary in a proceeding subject to the terms of the federal Indian child welfare act and in this chapter, the best interests of the Indian child may be served by placing the Indian child in accordance with the placement priorities expressed in this chapter. The legislature further finds that where placement away from the parent or Indian custodian is necessary for the child's safety, the state is committed to a placement that reflects and honors the unique values of the child's tribal culture and is best able to assist the Indian child in establishing, developing, and maintaining a political, cultural, social, and spiritual relationship with the child's tribe and tribal community.
>
> It is the intent of the legislature that this chapter is a step in clarifying existing laws and codifying existing policies and practices. This chapter shall not be construed to reject or eliminate current policies and practices that are not included in its provisions, RCW 13.38.030 Findings and intent.

The state law did provide clarification in many important respects. While other state courts across the country may still be embroiled in controversies over the interpretation of key provisions of the federal ICWA, Washington has straightforward state law to sidestep such controversies when Indian children are involved in placement proceedings.

Within the Washington Indian Child Welfare Act, the definitions section provides clear guidance on terms that had previously been subject to dissimilar treatment depending on the presiding judge or caseworker. For example, an express definition for "active efforts" and the minimum standards necessary to accomplish such efforts in reuniting an Indian family where a child is subject to a state placement proceeding is now available at RCW 13.38.040(1). Another significant provision of the state law was to address tribal exclusive jurisdiction. The state law largely tracks the ICWA provisions set forth at 25 U.S.C. § 1911(a). The following are the provisions from the Washington Indian Child Welfare Act, RCW 13.38.060:

> (1) An Indian tribe shall have exclusive jurisdiction over any child custody proceeding involving an Indian child who resides or is domiciled within the reservation of that tribe, unless the tribe has consented to the state's concurrent jurisdiction, the tribe has expressly declined to exercise its exclusive jurisdiction, or the state is exercising emergency jurisdiction in strict compliance with RCW 13.38.140.
> (2) If an Indian child is already a ward of a tribal court at the start of the child custody proceeding, the Indian tribe may retain exclusive jurisdiction, notwithstanding the residence or domicile of the child.

Subsection 1 limits state concurrent jurisdiction assumed under Public Law 280 to instances where a Tribe has expressly consented to the state's concurrent jurisdiction, otherwise the tribal court will have exclusive jurisdiction over a tribal child residing or domiciled on the Tribe's reservation. With this clarification, Indian child placement proceedings no longer require a full analysis of the state's delegated jurisdiction under Public Law 280 to determine whether an Indian child on his/her home reservation is subject to a state court proceeding or is under the jurisdiction of the local tribal court.

Each state may enact its own version of the Indian Child Welfare Act to provide uniform application by state agencies and courts. Washington serves as a recent model of this process. California, West's Ann. Cal. Fam. Code § 170, and Iowa, I.C.A. § 232B.1, have also incorporated provisions of the federal ICWA into state law. It should be noted that problems may still arise in these states interpreting the state law. For example in the 2008 case, *In the Interest of N.N.E.* 752 N.W.2d 1 (2008), the Iowa Supreme Court held that the Iowa state

ICWA's placement provisions were unconstitutional in a voluntary termination of parental rights proceeding by finding that under the federal ICWA the placement preferences could be disregarded on a finding of "good cause" which was not available under the Iowa ICWA, I.C.A. §232B.9.

Another trend developed in the late 1980s has been to apply a standard known as the "existing Indian family" doctrine to allow state court judges to evaluate whether the Indian parent(s) of the child met the state judge's definition of an Indian family as a prerequisite for following the ICWA provisions. State court judges finding that the parent(s) did not culturally participate in their tribal heritage could then rule that there was no concern for the ICWA to address in placing the Indian child in a non-Indian home. This doctrine has been severely criticized for the subjective discretion of state court judges to define "Indian families" and add new requirements to the federal law, but remains active in some state court jurisdictions. For example, the Indiana Supreme Court has upheld the "existing Indian family" doctrine in the 1988 case *Matter of Adoption of T.R.M.*, 525 N.E.2d 298, and the lower state courts continue to follow that decision. Tennessee state courts also apply the doctrine following the Tennessee Court of Appeals decision in the case, *In re Morgan*, No. 02A01-9608-CH-00206, 1997 WL 716880 (Tenn. Ct. App. Nov. 19, 1997).

There has been another very recent trend in some jurisdictions to abandon this doctrine. In 2004, the Oklahoma Supreme Court determined that the doctrine "was no longer viable" for cases involving application of the ICWA in the state court case, *In the Matter of Baby Boy L.*, 103 P.3d 1099. Kansas state courts were the first to develop the doctrine and in 2009 the Kansas Supreme Court expressly rejected its further application in the case, *In re A.J.S.*, 204 P.3d 543.

Further, many states have passed laws known as "Safe Haven Acts," which give immunity from criminal prosecution to any parent(s) or legal guardian who(m) abandons a child to a state agency or medical facility. The standard provisions under these state laws provide that no identifying information can be required from the parent about the child. Without identifying information, the provisions of the ICWA can be easily circumvented when the abandoned child is an Indian child. Resolving the intersection between state safe haven laws and the federal mandates of the ICWA will require on-going communication between state, tribal and federal agencies.

8. The Bureau of Indian Affairs Guidelines on the Indian Child Welfare Act

On the federal level, the Bureau of Indian Affairs (BIA) has published guidelines as direction to state courts on the application of the ICWA. Appearing in 67584 Federal Register Vol. 44 No. 228 on Monday, November 28, 1979, "The Bureau of Indian Affairs, Guidelines for State Courts; Indian Custody Proceedings" (hereinafter, "BIA Guidelines") continue to be relevant and referenced in state court decisions. Most recently the BIA Guidelines were relied upon by the U.S. Supreme Court in the *Adoptive Couple v. Baby Girl* 2013 decision interpreting the parental rights termination provisions of the ICWA. The "BIA Guidelines" expand on some of the provisions of the ICWA and provide the federal agency's interpretation on some key terms of the federal law.

For example, the Indian Child Welfare Act does not address the situation where an Indian child is enrolled in one Tribe and eligible for enrollment in another Tribe or where the child is not enrolled in any Tribe, but is eligible for enrollment in several Tribes. The "BIA Guidelines" contain direction to contact only the Tribe where the child is an enrolled member in the first situation and in the second, directs that all Tribes where the child is eligible for enrollment receive notice of the placement proceeding, "BIA Guidelines B.2. Determination of Indian Child's Tribe."

One of the most expansive interpretations provided in the "BIA Guidelines" concerns the term "good cause" as applied to determine that "good cause" exists to halt transfer of the child placement proceeding from state to tribal court. The Indian Child Welfare Act does not define what is "good cause" — the standard necessary to prevent the child's case from being transferred to the child's tribal court, 25 U.S.C. § 1911(b). In Section C.3(b) Determination of Good Cause to the Contrary, the "BIA Guidelines" provide a list for a state court judge to consider to determine whether the Indian child placement proceeding should not be transferred to the child's tribal court.

> b. Good cause not to transfer this proceeding may exist if any of the following circumstances exists:
>
> (i) The proceeding was at an advanced stage when the petition to transfer was received and the petitioner did not file the petition promptly after receiving notice of the hearing.
>
> (ii) The Indian child is over twelve years of age and objects to the transfer.

(iii) The evidence necessary to decide the case could not be adequately presented in the tribal court without undue hardship to the parties or the witnesses.

(iv) The parents of a child over five years of age are not available and the child has had little or no contact with the child's tribe or members of the child's tribe.

b.[sic] Socio-economic conditions and the perceived adequacy of tribal or Bureau of Indian Affairs social services or judicial systems may not be considered in a determination that good cause exists.

c. The burden of establishing good cause to the contrary shall be on the party opposing the transfer.

The basis for the factors listed are not supported by any explanation in the "BIA Guidelines" and seem to contradict the federal trust responsibility to Indian Tribes by articulating numerous ways to block transfer of an Indian child placement proceeding, including by determining that a child over the age of five "has had little or no contact with the child's tribe or members of the child's tribe."

The incorrectly lettered section contains two subsection "b"s. The second subsection b. does address part of the legislative history that led to the passage of the Indian Child Welfare Act. The perception of inadequate socio-economic conditions in Indian homes by state social workers or judges is expressly disavowed as a basis to block transfer of the proceeding to a tribal court.

Another provision of the "BIA Guidelines" establishes a right for an adult adoptee eighteen years or older to request from the state court the person's tribal affiliations. Section G.2(c) Adult Adoptee Rights provides: "[w]here state law prohibits revelation of the identity of the biological parent, assistance of the Bureau of Indian Affairs shall be sought where necessary to help an adoptee who is eligible for membership in a tribe establish that right without breaching the confidentiality of the record." Further in Section G.4, state courts are required to establish a recordkeeping location for all Indian child placement proceeding records and have them available "within seven days of a request by an Indian child's tribe or the Secretary [of the Interior]." These provisions support the return to tribal communities of Indians adopted out of Indian homes pursuant to state court proceedings.

E. Tribal Law and Tribal Families

Tribal governments may enact tribal laws on a wide variety of subjects that support tribal families and tribal values. The tribal value of gaining knowledge and wisdom is supported by tribal laws requiring children to attend school and holding parents responsible for truancy or excessive absences during the school year. Child protection and juvenile codes serve to translate tribal values into the societal norms enforceable in tribal communities to guide and protect the Tribe's youth.

1. Tribal Law and Domestic Relations

Social cohesion as a tribal value is enhanced with tribal laws that recognize legal unions in marriage. Marriage licenses are issued by tribal courts and marriage ceremonies take place in tribal courts. Tribal courts are employed to handle marriage dissolutions, child custody matters in the event of divorce or death of the child's parents, and property distribution as a result of a divorce. Recently, the traditions of same-sex marriage have been passed into official tribal law in several tribal communities. The Coquille Tribe of Oregon legalized same-sex marriage in May 2009 and the Suquamish Tribe of Washington in August 2011. In many pre-Christian tribal communities, same-sex couples were viewed as an important part of the community. The transgender and/or intersex individual was referred to in some tribal traditions as a "two-spirit" person with special spiritual gifts to assist the tribal community.

a. Tribal Communities and Domestic Violence

Also in support of healthy tribal families, tribal codes include provisions to address, appropriately punish and rehabilitate those engaging in the abuse of family members. Domestic violence laws may apply to any family member or may be written in separate codes to address particular family relationships. Spousal abuse and intimate relationship partner abuse are often the focus of tribal domestic violence protection laws. Elder abuse laws may also be enacted to protect the senior members of families from injury and harm. A tribal legislature may broadly define those protected by domestic violence provisions as simply "household members."

An Indian victim of domestic violence in a tribal community may seek a temporary protection order by filing a petition with the tribal court on an emergency basis. The temporary order will be enforceable by tribal law enforcement on tribal lands against an Indian defendant named in the order. The tribal court will schedule a hearing on the temporary order to allow for the alleged victim and defendant to each present testimony and evidence on whether the order should become a permanent protection order or should be dismissed. The hearing will often lead to other family law filings if the parties are married or have children together. Violation of a civil protection order may result in criminal prosecution if the tribal law provides for this in the criminal domestic violence laws.

Tribal Nations are increasingly dedicating funding and prioritization to domestic violence shelters for victims, counseling services for those involved in domestic violence, and rehabilitative services for perpetrators. Intertwined with issues of domestic violence may be substance abuse issues, lack of anger management skills, mental health issues, and other issues. Tribal courts are in a position to order a wide variety of program attendance and community service engagement for tribal members to resolve domestic violence situations in a holistic manner. In some instances, Tribal Wellness Courts have been established to bring community services into the lives of tribal members dealing with a host of issues.

As discussed in Chapter 3 Criminal Jurisdiction in Indian Country, creating safe tribal communities often involves navigating jurisdictional issues for the proper law enforcement and court authority to address the actions of an alleged perpetrator. When the alleged perpetrator is non-Indian, then tribal law enforcement and tribal courts are challenged to handle the domestic violence situation without local county and state partnerships. Tribal courts may order civil sanctions to a non-Indian perpetrator such as exclusion from tribal lands, civil fines or ordering participation in rehabilitative service programs. Due to the limitations on tribal criminal prosecution of non-Indians, cooperation with state law enforcement and courts is necessary to fully resolve such situations and hold accountable a non-Indian committing domestic violence acts against an Indian woman or Indian man on tribal lands and/or in tribal communities. In meeting these challenges, some tribal government officials have entered into agreements with local state officials to provide for recognition of tribal orders in state courts and vice versa.

With the 2013 amendments to the provisions in the Indian Civil Rights Act allowing for "special tribal domestic violence" jurisdiction, Tribes may choose to meet the federal requirements to assert jurisdiction over non-Indians committing domestic violence in the tribal community. There are significant requirements for a tribal judicial system to meet which will involve a weighing of advantages and disadvantages on these new provisions. See Chapter 3 for a fuller discussion of these amendments.

b. Mental Health and Substance Abuse Issues in Tribal Communities

In dealing with the changing eras of U.S. Indian policies, the vast majority of tribal families have experienced intergenerational poverty, dealt with racism, and experienced severe cultural transition and trauma. As tribal governments have rebuilt community infrastructure through social services and tribal courts, a priority has been to assist family members with mental health issues and/or who suffer from the effects of substance abuse. Many Tribal Nations have developed a tribal drug court program and/or a tribal wellness court program that is available to address all of the issues arising when a family is in crisis through ordering family members to attend substance abuse programs or mental health counseling programs. Often these services become necessary after a child neglect or abuse proceeding has been brought against parents in crisis. Tribal programs can be structured around the traditional tribal values that re-align families with the parenting and lifestyle practices known prior to the government boarding school era. Thus, these types of individual and family services can provide healing over generations and a return to wellness in tribal family life.

Checkpoints

- The domestic sphere of tribal law is an area where tribal values, culture and wisdom form the core. Tribal courts generally have exclusive authority in handling domestic issues occurring on tribal lands involving American Indians.

- Due to the U.S. Indian policy of assimilation, tribal members have suffered from the removal of children from tribal homes and federal conditioning to alter tribal culture and lifeways. Many tribal governments have prioritized protection of tribal languages, tribal knowledge, and tribal education systems to remedy the traumas from that policy era.

- The federal Indian Child Welfare Act (ICWA) was enacted to remedy cross-cultural misunderstandings of state agencies towards tribal families and provide a transfer process for cases involving placement of Indian children from state courts to tribal courts. Some states have passed their own state laws to further implement the provisions of the ICWA.

- Tribal family law continues to develop to address contemporary needs of tribal families. Tribal Wellness Courts are a current trend in addressing family issues in a holistic manner.

Chapter 7

Natural Resources in Indian Country

Roadmap

- Learn about the extensive role of the U.S. Department of the Interior in the management and leasing of tribal lands to utilize surface and subsurface resources.

- Learn about the engagement in environmental protection policies for water, air, and land by Tribal Nations in collaboration with the U.S. Environmental Protection Agency.

- Understand the basis of treaty hunting, fishing and gathering rights for tribal citizens and the continuing relevance of such rights.

- Understand the growing energy industry in Indian Country and the trend in federal laws that support the industry.

There are vast natural resource holdings throughout Indian country, from land, water, and timber, to a variety of subsurface estates with known and potential economic development viability. Because these resources are located within the only land base retained by Tribes, there are significant environmental and ecological concerns.

This chapter will cover natural resource development and management. For a full understanding of the material, readers should cross-reference this discussion with Chapter 2: "American Indian Property Law," Chapter 4: "Tribal Government, Civil Jurisdiction and Regulation," and Chapter 9: "Sacred Sites and Cultural Property Protection," as there is significant overlap within these areas.

A. United States as Trustee for Tribal Natural Resources

The federal government's allocation and reallocation of land and natural resources has shaped much of federal Indian law and policy. In some eras, the federal government has actively terminated tribal property rights or limited tribal holdings to smaller and smaller territories. On the other hand, the federal government has played an active role in protecting tribal natural resources from acquisitions by third parties, including the implementation of federal restraints on alienation that have ensured unencumbered tribal property interests. As a result of federal restraints on alienation, state taxation and regulation of tribal natural resources is generally prohibited. The development of natural resources inside Indian Country is generally a matter of federal law because the United States is typically the legal title holder of tribal natural resource estates, with the United States acting as a trustee for the beneficiary Tribe or individual Indian owner. Although property interests have been taken from Tribes without their consent and redistributed to third parties, as with the Surplus Lands Acts of the late 1800s and early 1900s, most forms of natural resources reallocations have been implemented in a more subtle fashion. As the trustee of tribal lands and natural resources, the United States has long exercised leasing power over both the surface and subsurface holdings of Tribes. With this power, the United States has exercised the power to approve oil and gas and other mineral production with or without tribal consent. This power also includes the authority of the federal government to grant easements across tribal land for roads, pipeline construction and maintenance, utilities, and other projects. While the trustee is theoretically charged with always acting in the best interest of the beneficiary, there is considerable room for abuse and lack of accountability that creates a precarious relationship between Tribes, individual Indians and the United States in this arena. This relationship is, without a doubt, one of the more contentious aspects of the modern government-to-government relationship between Tribes and the United States Department of Interior, which is charged in most instances with administrative control in this area.

When a natural resource is available for development, the United States, as the trustee, negotiates the terms of the development agreement, including bonus payments, royalty rates, and other compensation. In many instances, the compensation that has been negotiated for the Tribes by the United States has resulted in rates of return well below the competitive market values for the same natural resources.

Although modern federal legislation and regulations tend to place more control in tribal decision-making, including the power for Tribes to be the business entities in their own natural resource development and marketing, the federal government continues to play a significant role in leasing and in the collection of royalties and other compensation. Depending on the natural resource at issue, the United States plays a daily role in the management and administration of tribal natural resources as a duty imposed by federal statute.

Although the tribal natural resources arena is an area with many documented federal abuses, it is also an area where the federal government has been more aggressive in ensuring tribal autonomy than in some other areas. The federal Environmental Protection Agency (EPA), for example, is one of the few federal agencies that has viewed Tribes as having the capacity to self-regulate like states when it comes to regulations governing pollution control. The federal EPA views Indian Country to be a marker of territorial jurisdiction and does not limit its view of tribal regulatory power as limited to only those lands that are owned by the Tribe or its citizens/members. By its very nature, environmental regulation cannot be effective if regulation is treated as a checkerboard of land tenure patterns with the Tribe regulating one tract of land and the state, perhaps with less stringent environmental controls, regulating the parcel of land next door.

1. Leasing of Tribal Lands

The Secretary of the Interior is charged with approving the leasing of tribal lands, both in the case of lands held by the tribal government as the owner and allotted lands, provided the lands are held in federal trust status, 25 U.S.C. § 415. Extensive regulations operate depending on the type of lease sought, 25 C.F.R. Part 162.00. The maximum time-period for a lease is controlled by federal statutes and regulations, and will depend largely upon the type of natural resource at issue.

The Secretary's approval of a lease is a federal action that implicates the National Environmental Policy Act (NEPA) and requires a study of environmental consequences of the federal action. Although such review is typically advantageous to the Tribes to ensure sustainability of resources and minimize environmental degradation, NEPA is often viewed by the Tribes as an undue bureaucratic obstacle to development. When Tribes are considering whether to retain a tract of land in fee status, or request that that federal government take the land into trust, NEPA considerations and the time delay often associated with such review is a critical factor in making that decision. If the Tribe retains fee title to the land, the Tribe is free to lease its land on its own initiative, without federal approval. Once land or natural resources are leased on trust lands with the requisite federal approval, the Department of Interior takes an active role in lease management. The federal government, as trustee, has the duty to ensure lease compliance which includes ensuring that the lease terms are complied with by all third parties.

2. Duties of the Federal Trustee

As the trustee, the United States has the power to foreclose a lease for failure to make payments and the duty to collect payments, including the duty to account for the natural resources removed according to the terms of the lease. As the trustee, the United States owes a fiduciary obligation to the Tribes or individual Indian property owners and may be held accountable for damages for violation of the trust responsibility.

Enforcement claims in breach of trust cases are brought against the executive branch, typically the Secretary of the Interior, over the conduct of the Bureau of Indian Affairs. The origin of the trust responsibility is multi-faceted and either comes from the contractual relationship between the Tribe and United States in treaties, from an implicit understanding of the guardian-ward relationship the United States declared to take on over the Tribes, or it derives expressly from provisions of statute or regulations.

Tribes are frequently frustrated with the lack of clarity with respect to the trust responsibility and conflicting language in federal court cases that declare that the United States, as a trustee, does not have the same duty one may expect from a trustee in the private sector, such as a bank.

For instance, the United States is said to have only a "limited" trust relationship with tribal allottees following the General Allotment Act, whereby the United States required the division of tribal property to individual Indians. In order for there to be a more "complete" trust duty, a specific statute or regulation which affirmatively requires the federal government to take action is required, and then the United States can be held accountable for failing to affirmatively act.

In the management of timber, specific duties are assigned which would invoke an enforceable trust, such as the management of sustainable yields. This was held to be true in the *United States v. Mitchell*, 463 U.S. 206 (1983) (*Mitchell II*) decision where the U.S. Supreme Court upheld a tribal claim for breach of the trust responsibility in failing to properly manage the timber on the Quinault Indian Reservation. In that case, the Court held that it was significant that the U.S. role was almost daily supervision of every aspect of the tribal timber operations thereby, creating an enforceable trust duty subject to monetary damages for a breach of that duty. The fact that the United States approves a lease, however, does not necessarily mean that the United States could be held accountable for breach of trust if the price for the lease is below market value.

The most notorious breach of trust lawsuit against the United States, *Cobell v. Salazar*, 573 F.3d 808 (D.C. Cir. 2009) (Cobell XXII), was a class action lawsuit that led to a 3.4 billion dollar settlement regarding the administration of assets from natural resource development and management of tribal trust lands on behalf of individual Indian owners. The settlement called for a comprehensive evaluation of federal trust administration of Indian resources, both hard assets and the funds that are administered from appropriation of natural resources. As a result of the lawsuit and settlement agreement, reform recommendations are forthcoming. In *Cobell*, the federal government had been the repository of funds collected on behalf of the individual allottees from mineral leasing and other income sources. After collecting the funds on behalf of the allottees the United States was unable to provide a reliable accounting to the individual account holders and the settlement represented the best estimate of monies owed. *Cobell* provides the classic example of how individual Indian landowners are tied to a system that, to date, fails to meet their needs. Lands are held by the United States, and consequently, monies from the sale, lease and development of natural resources are administered by the federal government down to the collection, withdrawal and oversight of funds. Although opportunities for tribal control at the local level are available, and more and more Tribes have taken on the role of natural resources and property management by opening tribal realty offices, the Tribes are limited in carrying out the necessary federal functions by delegation. A Tribe is not free to create a freely standing and more efficient administrative office because the United States continues to be the legal title-holder, absent legislative reform to the contrary. Further, absent legislative mechanisms that ensure that the lands and natural resources will not become subject to state taxation and regulations, Tribes are reluctant to support a system whereby the United States could simply walk away from the current broken system and thereby escape accountability as a trustee.

B. Water Rights and Air Regulation

The ability to ensure an adequate water supply, both in terms of quality and quantity is critical to tribal community sustainability. Indian water rights have their origin in the time immemorial use of water, the creation of the reservation systems, or other scenarios where the United States, either by treaty, executive order or statute, set aside a permanent homeland for a tribe as a recognized territory. Although rights to water were typically not expressly reserved in such documents, federal courts have ruled that it would have been inconceivable that Tribes would have been able to maintain a community, including domestic activities, resources development and agricultural pursuits, without sufficient water to support those needs. As such, Tribes enjoy an implied reservation of water rights along with rights to land and territory. In the West, where water can be scarce, a Tribe's water rights are preserved as to the dates of time immemorial use for hunting and fishing rights acknowledged in treaties. In the U.S. Supreme Court case, *United States v. Winans*, 198 U.S. 371 (1905), the Court stated that Tribes reserve all rights not expressly waived or relinquished in treaties. In the water rights context, this translates to reserving water used for hunting and fishing purposes since time immemorial.

For most other purposes, the creation of the reservation sets the date for the Indian water right as set forth in the U.S. Supreme Court case, *Winters v. United States*, 207 U.S. 564 (1908). In the western system of prior appropriation, that prioritizes water rights in order of "first in time, first in right," the *Winters* doctrine established Tribes as among the most senior, and therefore prioritized water rights holders in a given area. Should the Tribe have sufficient water to meet its own needs, tribal water rights may be leased to individuals, including non-Indians, provided the United States as trustee, approves and manages such leases.

In terms of environmental viability, tribal regulation of water has been upheld and supported by the federal government through the Clean Water Act, 33 U.S.C. § 1377. The Clean Water Act was amended to include a provision for Tribes to be treated as states, referred to as "TAS" status, in terms of setting water quality standards within tribal boundaries. Many Tribes maintain their own tribal EPA office that regulates water within the Tribe's territory including the issuance of permits and establishment of tribal water quality standards. This is one area where tribal regulatory power can have off-reservation reach. If the Tribe sets water quality standards that are higher than a state or municipality located upstream, the other jurisdictions may have to adopt more stringent water quality standards to ensure that the water meets the tribal standards when the stream enters the tribal jurisdiction. Similar to the Clean Water Act, the federal Safe Drinking Water Act, 42 U.S.C. § 300j-11(b), includes the ability of Tribes to be treated as states to set safe drinking water quality standards within tribal boundaries.

Conflicts over the extent of Indian water rights, although federal in nature, are adjudicated in state courts because the United State has consented to this forum pursuant to the 1952 McCarran Amendment, codified at 43 U.S.C. § 666. Water rights adjudications typically take years to resolve and have been the source of some conflict between the Tribes and the United States as the trustee. As the trustee, the federal government is the party representing the

Tribes in the enforcement of water rights, but the federal government may have competing interests, even from sub-agencies within the Department of the Interior or from the United States representing the interests of other Tribes or owners within the same litigation. A national online e-repository of Native American Water Settlements is maintained jointly by the University of Idaho College of Law and the Utton Center at the University of New Mexico School of Law, available at: http://repository.unm.edu/handle/1928/21727.

Finally, the federal Clean Air Act, 42 U.S.C. § 7401 et seq., has the strongest delegation of federal environmental regulatory authority to tribal governments. Under 42 U.S.C. § 7601(d), tribal governments may establish and enforce EPA-approved tribal implementation plans ("TIPs") for air quality within tribal boundaries. Within the federal legislation is a process for tribal governments and state governments to resolve issues that may arise in re-designating air quality across regions, 42 U.S.C. § 7474(e). Air as a natural resource is becoming increasingly protected by tribal governments as a result of the opportunity for the federal regulatory delegation under the Clean Air Act.

The federal law dealing with the regulation of solid waste and dump sites is the Resource Conservation and Recovery Act (RCRA), 42 U.S.C. § 6901 et seq. While other federal environmental statutes have been amended to allow the Tribes-as-states designation, RCRA does not include this provision. The default authority for environmental regulation under RCRA is the federal government on tribal lands. Tribes may collaborate and seek grants from the EPA for specific programs on handling and providing clean up of solid waste on tribal lands.

C. Hunting, Fishing, and Gathering Rights

Similar to water rights, it is presumed that tribal territorial rights included the implied right to sustainability in the use rights of hunting, fishing and gathering. It would have been inconceivable that Tribes would have agreed to a smaller and fixed territory without the right to use the resources within the territory, and to make use of the resources without the infringement of outside regulations, particularly regulation from the states. Tribal hunting and fishing rights have been protected to such a great extent that federal courts recognized continued treaty rights in individual Indians even after the United States no longer recognized the political existence of a tribe, as a federally recognized tribal entity. For example in the *Menominee Tribe of Indians v. United States*, 391 U.S. 404 (1968) case, the U.S. Supreme Court held that treaty hunting and fishing rights survived for the tribal members after the federal termination of the Menominee Tribe.

Outside of a Tribe's current territory, it is possible that these use rights continue, even if the Tribe has expressly waived other rights in subsequent treaties. Tribes have successfully asserted use rights, even on private third-party lands, where treaties preserved the rights for Indians to hunt and fish in the places that they traditionally used for such purposes prior to removal. In these instances, it becomes a fact question, through the development of the historical record, whether the lands at issue were lands that the Tribe exercised such rights. A good example of a contemporary decision upholding off-reservation or "usufructuary" treaty rights is *Minnesota v. Mille Lacs Band of Chippewa Indians*, 562 U.S. 172 (1999), where the U.S. Supreme Court interpreted the 1837 Treaty with the Mille Lacs Band and concluded that no subsequent actions on the part of the federal government had abolished the off-reservation treaty rights to hunt, fish and gather on the lands ceded by the Tribe.

Modern conflicts have centered not around the right to access lands for such purposes, but whether, based on a treaty right, how tribal hunting and fishing is to be construed against competing hunting and fishing rights. In turn, what entity has the right to regulate hunting and fishing through the requirements of licensing or regulation of seasons or quantity restrictions become significant for the exercise of tribal treaty rights.

Tribal governments maintain the exclusive right to regulate hunting, fishing and gathering on tribally owned lands, and to condition the entry upon such lands by tribal licensing requirements or other such regulations. Tribal power in this instance applies to both Indians and non-Indians. Where Tribes no longer maintain the right to exclude, however, tribal power to regulate non-Indian hunting and fishing will not be exclusively recognized. For example in *Montana v. United States*, 450 U.S. 544 (1981), the U.S. Supreme Court held that the Crow Tribe did not have the authority to ban all hunting by non-Indians on privately owned fee lands within the Crow Reservation's boundaries. Thus, states and local non-tribal governments typically require licensing and apply seasonal limits on fee lands, even if inside tribal territorial boundaries.

Specific treaty provisions are worth mentioning to demonstrate the ongoing enforcement of treaty rights. As the United States sought to expand westward, Isaac Stevens was appointed territorial governor of Washington, which included the position of Superintendent of Indian Affairs. As territorial governor, Stevens negotiated many treaties to provide for non-Indian settlement in the region. One feature of the so-called "Stevens Treaties" was the insistence of various Tribes in the Northwest to include the right of fishing "at all usual and accustomed grounds." In the Stevens Treaties, these fishing rights were to be exercised "in common with all citizens of the Territory." The U.S. Supreme Court interpreted this treaty language in *Washington v. Washington State Com-*

mercial Passenger Fishing Vessel Association, 443 U.S. 658 (1979) and found that the tribal parties retained a maximum of fifty percent allocation of the annual fish harvest to allow Indian fishers a moderate living standard.

For off-reservation regulatory matters of the fish runs, the states are to consult with treaty Tribes prior to adversely impacting treaty rights. The states continue to exercise regulatory powers for conservation purposes over Indians and non-Indians alike. If a state regulation is not necessary for conservation purposes, and the regulation would otherwise be inconsistent with treaty-based rights, the state powers would be preempted in favor of the treaty right. In extreme circumstances, state powers could potentially result in a complete ban relative to a certain species. Tribes have increasingly developed scientific expertise in the areas of the country where they exert off-reservation treaty rights to engage in such conservation decisions.

D. Energy and Resource Development

Consistent with the economic development discussion in Chapter 5: "Tribal Business, Industries and Best Commercial Practices," Tribes have viewed the development of their natural resources as an economic priority and necessity but also as a decision which is complex for each community. In addition to the numerous federal law requirements which address leasing and development of various resources on tribal land, Tribes are becoming increasingly sophisticated in how they manage development as a matter of tribal law. Many Tribes, in addition to tribal EPA offices, maintain departments of natural resources, forestry, hunting and fishing agencies, and tribal agriculture departments which not only administer tribal programs aimed at promoting the tribal economy, but also serve as the regulatory body of first contact with federal and private partners. Further, since taxation of natural resources is an important part of the tribal tax base, tribal governments often create tribal tax commissions charged with overseeing severance taxes which are accessed from many energy development activities.

The evolution of federal statutory schemes in Indian Country, regardless of the natural resources at issue, typically started with a general statue such as the Mineral Leasing Act of 1920, which granted authority for the Department of the Interior to oversee development operations on federal public lands. Specific to Indian Country, the Indian Mineral Leasing Act of 1938, 25 U.S.C. §§ 396a–396g, was intended to extend greater authority to tribal governments in line with the Indian Reorganization Act of 1934, 25 U.S.C. § 465 et seq. Statutory reforms, particularly in the 1970s, continued a strong federal presence in the development of tribal resources, but with an eye toward a modern policy of protection of the environment and more flexibility in private and tribal business enterprise, increasing options for Tribes and creating more of an open market for federal leasing including agreements for Tribes to have more control over long term planning. The Indian Mineral Development Act of 1982, 25 U.S.C. §§ 2101–2108, included greater flexibility for tribal governments to act as partners with third parties or engage in other arrangements, rather than straight leasing agreements. These federal regulatory schemes continued to expand to include not only the traditional oil, gas, and coal leases, but also geothermal, wind, and developing technologies.

Under the Energy Policy Act of 2005, the Indian Tribal Energy Development and Self-Determination Act was passed allowing for a Tribe to submit an energy development plan for overall project approval to the Department of Interior. Once approved, then the tribal government will have the authority to negotiate all related agreements to implement the energy development project. The Department of the Interior is required to create processes to encourage increased tribal autonomy including the above-mentioned tribal energy resource agreements (TERAs) in which the Tribes approve and manage their own leases and agreements for energy development. It is the continuing trend to provide more tribal control and more meaningful self-determination in the energy development area.

As this book goes to press, the Department of Interior is implementing the Helping Expedite and Advance Responsible Tribal Homeownership (HEARTH) Act of 2012, which allows Tribes, in limited instances, to lease lands that are restricted against alienation without the approval of the Department of the Interior. Although the legislation's applicability is limited to surface rights, it is another step toward recognizing tribal autonomy to develop tribal leasing regulations. The Tribe's leasing regulations, however, are not self-executing under the Act and cannot be fully implemented until approved by the Secretary of the Interior.

In this era of Indian self-determination, federal legislation regarding tribal natural resources is beginning to provide options for tribal government to assert greater managerial authority and decision-making in this field. In meeting the advancing technologies and opportunities over natural resource development, conservation, and protection, tribal governments are moving forward and acquiring the technological, scientific, and legal skills and expertise to implement tribal plans in these areas.

Checkpoints

- Tribal natural resources on trust lands are under the management authority of the U.S. Department of the Interior. An extensive body of federal regulations has been created on the leasing, extraction, and approval processes for commercial use of tribal natural resources.

- The federal trust responsibility to tribal governments and individuals provides guidance on federal decision-making regarding tribal natural resource extraction and usage.

- A strong relationship of collaboration has been maintained between many tribal governments and the U.S. Environmental Protection Agency (EPA). Several major federal environmental protection statutes have been amended and implemented by the EPA recognizing tribal governments as states for federal programs and processes.

- Tribal governments have invested heavily in the protection of treaty hunting, fishing and gathering rights. Tribal natural resource departments supply scientific expertise to tribal conservation efforts.

- Recent federal laws have supported the U.S. Indian policy of self-determination by providing for greater tribal authority over natural resource and energy development.

Chapter 8

Tribal-State Relations

Roadmap

- Know that the primary relationship was established between the U.S. federal government and Tribal Nations.
- Learn about the history of relations between state governments seeking full territorial sovereignty and tribal governments asserting federal treaties to recognize tribal territories.
- Understand there are important common areas of concern shared by tribal and state governments allowing for diplomatic and cooperative relations.

Tribal government and state government relations occur within the scope and history of federal Indian law. Under the U.S. Constitution, individual states were eligible to seek admission to the union pursuant to Article IV, Section 3, after organizing as territories. The territories were formed after treaties were entered into by U.S. federal officials with Tribal Nations to allow for settlement in lands ceded under the treaties. Thus, the states created after the original thirteen in the United States often were required to recognize in the federal admission act that the newly established governing body would not interfere with reserved Indian lands or rights.

An example of this language in an act of admission from the Kansas-Nebraska Act of 1854 was as follows:

> ... Provided further, that nothing in this act contained shall be construed to impair the rights of person or property now pertaining to the Indians in said territory, so long as such rights shall remain unextinguished by treaty between the United States and such Indians, or to include any territory which, by treaty with any Indian tribe, is not, without the consent of said tribe, to be included the territorial limits or jurisdiction of any state or territory; but all such territory shall be excepted out of the boundaries, and constitute no part of the territory of Nebraska, until said tribe shall signify their assent to the pres-

ident of the United States to be included within the said territory of Nebraska, or to affect the authority of the government of the United States to make any regulations respecting such Indians, their lands, property, or other rights by treaty, law or otherwise, which it would have been competent to the government to make if this act had never passed. 10 Stat. 277, Section 1.

This same boilerplate language was included in Section 19 of the Kansas-Nebraska Act for the limitations on the admission of Kansas to the Union. Other examples of the reserved rights of American Indians can be found in the enabling acts of many of the states joining the Union throughout the West. The enabling act to organize the states of Montana, North Dakota, South Dakota, and Washington, 25 Stat. 676, February 22, 1889, contained numerous provisions limiting state authority to tax Indians or Indian lands as well as similar language to the Kansas-Nebraska Act explicitly recognizing Indian treaty rights and lands as under the authority of federal law.

As state governments matured, tensions arose over respecting reserved Indian territories within the designated state boundaries. These tensions have been exacerbated at times by federal legislation pitting state and tribal governmental control against each other, such as through the passage of the General Allotment Act of 1887, codified at 25 U.S.C. § 331 (repealed), whereby Indian lands were re-designated as "surplus" and purchased as federal lands. These lands were then sold to settlers under state government jurisdiction within the boundaries of Indian reservations. Chapter 2: "American Indian Property Law" sets forth a fuller discussion of the allotment policy. Throughout this history, federal and state governmental tensions have also become highlighted in the area of federal Indian law with Tribal Nations seeking enforcement of agreements and treaties with each of these levels of the United States, the federal level and the state level.

A. Historical Tribal-State Relations

The Marshall Trilogy cases of the 1800s interpreting the U.S. Constitution's Commerce Clause provide the basis for the doctrine that the federal government preempts state government policy and law in Indian affairs. Expressly in *Worcester v. Georgia*, 31 U.S. (6 Pet.) 515 (1832), the U.S. Supreme Court held the treaties entered into between the federal government and the Cherokee Nation preempted the laws of the state of Georgia within the territory of the Cherokee Nation where those state laws seized tribal lands, sought to nullify tribal laws, and required a state license for non-Indians to reside within the tribal territory. In the opinion, Justice Marshall stated:

> The acts of the legislature of Georgia interfere forcibly with the relations established between the United States and the Cherokee nation, the regulation of which, according to the settled principles of our constitution, is committed exclusively to the government of the union, 31 U.S. at 520.

Thus, under federal Indian law as set forth by the U.S. Constitution and as interpreted by the U.S. Supreme Court, relations with tribal governments are the primary province of the federal government and not the individual state governments in the United States.

As a practical matter, the state governments are in frequent relations with tribal governments due to territorial proximity and the interrelationship with tribal citizens, who are also citizens of the United States and state governments. With passage of the 1924 Indian Citizenship Act, 43 Stat. 253 (June 2, 1924), any American Indian who had not become a citizen of the United States by a prior law did so with presumed state citizenship, both were then attached to the pre-existing tribal citizenship. Tribal-state relations run the spectrum from friendly cooperation from state governments to aggressive attempts to negate tribal sovereignty and assert state governmental control. Greater levels of cooperation in tribal-state relations may be reached where interests converge on both sides.

One of the most well-known statements on tribal-state relations was contained in the U.S. Supreme Court opinion, *U.S. v. Kagama,* 118 U.S. 375 (1886), where American Indians were characterized in a very negative light along with the attitudes of state citizens and governments toward American Indians.

> These Indian tribes *are* the wards of the nation. They are communities *dependent* on the United States, — dependent largely for their daily food; dependent for their political rights. They owe no allegiance to the states, and receive from them no protection. Because of the local ill feeling, the people of the states where they are found are often their deadliest enemies, 118 U.S. at 383–384 (emphasis in the original).

This Court opinion was written prior to the Indian Citizenship Act of 1924 and does not fully reflect tribal-state relations that have evolved since the late 1800s.

B. Contemporary Tribal-State Relations

In this chapter, the development of tribal-state relations will be explored in the key areas of: 1) state governmental Indian affairs commissions and tribal liaisons, 2) tribal-state relations and law enforcement; 3) tribal-state revenue agreements; and 4) tribal-state co-management agreements. Other areas of mutual interest exist beyond these key areas, such as family law matters including implementing the provisions of the federal Indian Child Welfare Act in state court proceedings involving Indian children and implementing the federal Temporary Assistance to Needy Families (TANF) provisions under state law formulas. The interaction between tribal sovereignty and state governmental authority continue to call for refined approaches with the call at times bringing governments together and at times falling on deaf ears.

Tribal governments operate from a sovereignty that pre-dates the establishment of the United States. With the formation of the United States and its component state governments, new governmental relations have become necessary between the local, state, and federal governments with tribal governments. Tribal governments must maintain relations with all of these levels of the United States government and seek acceptable agreements for matters that impact the tribal territory, tribal citizenry, and tribal interests.

1. State Governmental Indian Affairs Commissions and Tribal Liaisons

Due to the many points of contact between state governments and tribal governments, many state legislatures and governors have established formal Indian affairs commissions and tribal liaison positions to promote cooperation between the particular state and the area Tribal Nations. Some state Indian affairs councils are established by state law, which is the case for the following states: Alabama, Arizona, Colorado, Maryland, Massachusetts, Minnesota, and North Carolina, to name a few. Other states have taken a specific purpose for establishing tribal relations commissions. For example, Georgia has established by state law the Georgia Council on American Indian Concerns with a primary purpose of protecting Indian burial sites and archaeological sites. Kentucky has established the Kentucky Native American Heritage Commission to "recognize and promote Native American contributions and influence in Kentucky's history and culture," according to the Commission's web site.

Another step towards better intergovernmental relations is the creation of a tribal liaison position between state government and tribal government(s).

State governors may also appoint a cabinet level official in this role who has experience working with or in tribal communities. For example, in September 2011 California governor, Edmund Brown issued an Executive Order creating the position of Governor's Tribal Advisor in the Office of the Governor to strengthen collaboration and communication with the one hundred plus Tribal Nations in the state.

Within state governmental departments, tribal liaison positions facilitate cooperation between state government and tribal government(s) to apply for federal funding for projects that will benefit both state and tribal communities. Within the state transportation departments of California, Minnesota and Washington, tribal liaison positions are active to promote beneficial relations with tribal governments. In addition, often state environmental protection programs incorporate tribal liaison positions and boards to foster intergovernmental environmental protection plans. Michigan and New York both incorporate Native American affairs positions within their departments of family services. The state of Arizona may have the most extensive number of tribal liaisons working with various departments of state government, with forty such positions listed in the state tribal liaison directory.

In New Mexico, the state Indian Affairs Department (IAD) web site states that the department was founded in 2003 as the successor to the Office of Indian Affairs established in the 1950s. The IAD was "the first and only cabinet level state Indian affairs department in the nation," according to the web site. Furthermore, the goals of the IAD include on-going work to "set the standard for what is possible when state and tribal governments work together to address mutual concerns in respectful and positive dialogue between sovereign governments." There are twenty-two federally-recognized Tribes in New Mexico interacting with the state IAD.

2. Tribal-State Relations and Law Enforcement

As discussed in Chapter 3 Criminal Jurisdiction in Indian Country, tribal governments have primary criminal jurisdiction in the tribal territory with the exception of criminal activity perpetrated by non-Indians. Concurrent jurisdiction will exist either with the federal government by federal law or with state governments when there has been a federal delegation, such as in the Public Law 280 states. Federal delegation of criminal authority to state governments for Indians within Indian Country has had a significant impact on tribal-state relations where those delegations are in effect. The interaction between state law enforcement and tribal citizenry necessarily has increased with the delegations.

State law enforcement will also have authority in Indian Country where criminal activity involves only non-Indian on non-Indian crimes.

In recent years, there has been a reported epidemic of violence perpetrated against Native women. Those studying this epidemic have highlighted a perceived lack of state and federal prosecution of non-Indians committing assault and battery within Indian Country, thus imposing no consequences on non-Indian perpetrators. Tribal law enforcement officers lack authority over non-Indian perpetrators according to the U.S. Supreme Court decision in *Oliphant v. Suquamish Tribe*, 435 U.S. 191 (1978). With the passage of the 2010 Tribal Law and Order Act (TLOA), the offices of the U.S. Attorney General across the nation are to work more closely with tribal law enforcement and report on decisions to decline prosecutions for those investigated for possible criminal activity on reservations, 25 U.S.C. § 2809. In every federal district, the TLOA requires that at least one assistant United States Attorney will be appointed as the tribal liaison for the district, 25 U.S.C. § 2810. Further, the TLOA encouraged cooperation among state, tribal and local law enforcement under 25 U.S.C. § 2815 by authorizing the U.S. Attorney General to provide assistance when cooperative agreements are entered into at those governmental levels. The cooperative agreements may relate to topics of "mutual aid, hot pursuit of suspects, and cross-deputization."

Also, the 2013 amendments to the Indian Civil Rights Act with provisions for "special tribal domestic violence jurisdiction" may be an avenue for tribal governments to assert authority over non-Indians committing such violence against Indians on tribal lands. This is further discussed in Chapter 3 Criminal Jurisdiction in Indian Country.

Currently, state and county levels of coordination with tribal law enforcement varies from very collaborative to completely uncooperative. Due to the history of hostility expressed in the *Kagama* decision mentioned previously, both tribal citizens and state citizens may resist law enforcement from the other one's community enforcing laws and making arrests in their neighborhoods. However, the positives to be gained from joint law enforcement efforts can be very beneficial to the safety and protection of both tribal and state citizens. Examples of collaborative practices between tribal and state law enforcement include the development of cooperative agreements and cross-deputization agreements. The National Congress of American Indians (NCAI) web site under Tribal-State Relations contains a listing by state of law enforcement agreements entered into with tribal law enforcement departments.

One of the incentives for entering into cooperative agreements has been the upsurge in recent years of the illegal production, use, transportation and selling of methamphetamine occurring in Indian Country by non-Indians and

Indians. A 2006 survey, *National Methamphetamine Initiative Survey, The Status of the Methamphetamine Threat and Impact on Indian Lands,* indicated that responding tribal law enforcement departments identified the majority of methamphetamine entering their communities primarily from non-Indians (Hispanic, Caucasian, and African-Americans) and 90% of the departments indicated their department was in need of specialized training for criminal investigations involving this illegal substance. This report is available on the NCAI web site at: www.ncai.org/ncai/Meth/BIA_MethSurvey.pdf. Further, the respondents in the study reported on page 15 "significant increases in instances of domestic violence, burglary, assault, and child abuse as a direct result of methamphetamine use." Cooperation with other law enforcement agencies is absolutely necessary when illegal drug trafficking reaches Indian Country as tribal law enforcement departments generally lack authority over non-Indian traffickers, users or producers.

The operation of Class III gaming in tribal communities under tribal-state compacts has provided another opportunity for mutual law enforcement activities. The Indian Gaming Regulatory Act (IGRA) provides that gaming compacts may include express provisions on the prosecution of criminal activity in tribal gaming enterprises and on what criminal laws will apply in the gaming enterprise, 25 U.S.C. § 2710(d)(3)(C). By reaching an agreement, uncertainty and delay in response time by appropriate law enforcement personnel to handle immediate situations may be significantly decreased. In order for Tribal Nations to effectively operate businesses, law enforcement must be responsive to protect the patronage, enforce the applicable laws at the establishment, and have authority to handle any criminal situation that may arise.

In a variety of contexts, law enforcement authorities at the tribal, state and local level are engaging in mutual efforts to prevent harbors for criminal activity when jurisdictional lines are crossed. By allowing for cross-deputization agreements in tribal territories, tribal police officers can arrest and transfer non-Indians to the local state court system for prosecution and in turn, state and county officers can arrest and transfer Indians to the local tribal court system for prosecution. Cross-deputization agreements can assist in eliminating fugitive situations where perpetrators seek to hide from a particular jurisdiction, for instance where a warrant has been issued, by traveling to another jurisdiction. With proper training and shared interests in community safety, tribal and state law enforcement can work collaboratively for the good of Indian and non-Indians in areas where both live.

3. Tribal-State Revenue Agreements

Taxes and governmental income are the usual primary sources of revenue for any government in the United States to operate. State governments can acquire taxes and revenue from transactions occurring on tribal lands due to U.S. Supreme Court decisions on state taxation of non-tribal members doing business on tribal lands; federal laws on extraction of resources from tribal lands that include state taxation provisions; and the Tribal-State compacting process under the Indian Gaming Regulatory Act (IGRA) when revenue sharing is included. Some state governments have engaged in aggressive raids of tribal smoke shops, for instance, to seize cigarettes at the heart of tobacco tax disputes. In other instances, some state officials have applied strong-arm bargaining tactics pursuing revenue sharing agreements with Tribal Nations seeking Class III gaming which is only permitted when a Tribal-State gaming compact is entered into. In response, many tribal governments have preferred to go to the bargaining table and enter into a taxation or revenue sharing agreement rather than have violence erupt from state law enforcement raids in tribal communities or fighting contentious legal battles in federal courts with high expenditures and often adverse consequences to tribal sovereignty as a result.

a. Tribal-State Taxation Agreements

Since the late 1970s, U.S. Supreme Court decisions have allowed state governments concurrent taxing authority for goods purchased by non-members in tribal communities. The court decisions have arisen from the development of tribal businesses offering tobacco products and motor fuels which were frequented by non-Indians and Indians within tribal communities. For individual purchasers in Montana, the U.S. Supreme Court held in *Moe v. Confederated Salish and Kootenai Tribes,* 425 U.S. 463, 483 (1976) that "[t]he State's requirement that the Indian tribal seller collect a tax validly imposed on non-Indians is a minimal burden designed to avoid the likelihood that in its absence non-Indians purchasing from the tribal seller will avoid payment of a concededly lawful tax." Unlike other governmental jurisdictions with taxes that apply straight across the board to all purchasers, tribal governments must determine the citizenship status of the purchaser to manage this concurrent state taxation scheme. As for state taxation on fuel sales to tribal gas stations, the U.S. Supreme Court in *Wagnon v. Prairie Band Potawatomi,* 546 U.S. 95 (2003) held that a Kansas state tax with the legal incidence falling on a non-tribal member motor fuels distributor was validly applied on sales on tribal lands.

One of the difficulties resulting from this line of federal cases is that generally state government has no ability to collect taxes on tribal lands without the cooperation of tribal government and tribal businesses. In *Oklahoma Tax Commission v. Citizen Band of Potawatomi Indian Tribe,* 498 U.S. 505, 514, the U.S. Supreme Court informed state governments that the options they may pursue to collect state taxes for cigarette sales to non-tribal members on tribal lands include: holding tribal officers liable for money damages in federal court, seizing unstamped cigarettes off the reservation, assessing state taxes before the cigarettes reach the reservation, seeking federal authorizing legislation to enter tribal lands to collect taxes or entering into tax agreements with tribal governments. When tribal governments resist the collection of state taxes on goods purchased on tribal lands, some states have sent in state troopers to seize cigarettes and arrest tribal business owners and employees. Federal officers have also raided tobacco shops on tribal lands under federal warrants for failure to apply state taxes. As of 2013, there have been many state and federal raids on tribal tobacco shops over the last ten years in New York, Oklahoma, Oregon, Washington, and in other states.

A well-known example occurred on July 14, 2003, when Rhode Island state troopers executed a state warrant on a tribal smoke shop operated by the Narragansett Tribe. The shop had been open for two days when state law enforcement descended to seize cigarettes being sold without state taxes applied. In the violent clash that ensued, tribal leaders were arrested as local television news crews reported on the situation. Instead of resorting to a civil lawsuit, the state leadership had sent in "51 police officers, including a SWAT team and a police dog, to enforce tobacco laws" according to testimony in the state cases seeking prosecution of seven tribal members for resisting arrest as reported in the national newspaper USA Today on February 29, 2008. Ultimately, the federal Court of Appeals upheld the right of the state to collect taxes on cigarette sales to non-tribal members by executing the state warrant based upon the Rhode Island Indian Claims Settlement Act of 1978 in the *Narragansett Indian Tribe v. Rhode Island,* 449 F.3d 16 (1st Cir. 2006) decision. Furthermore, seven prosecutions were brought against tribal members with four acquitted of all charges and three convicted of disorderly or assault charges in the aftermath of the state police raid.

To avoid the protracted litigation and prosecution of tribal citizens that may result from resistance to the imposition of concurrent taxing authority by state governments, tribal governments have negotiated tax agreements, particularly for tobacco sales and motor fuel sales. The Oklahoma Indian Affairs Commission maintains a web page listing tribal-state tax agreements for tobacco sales and motor fuel sales with many of the tribal governments in the state. As an example of the common text of such agreements, the Montana Department of Revenue has posted a draft proposed tobacco tax agreement with the Northern Cheyenne Tribe on its web site, dated November 9, 2011, providing that the state collect one tax prior to tobacco sales on the reservation and will then remit to the Tribe on a quarterly basis only the amount of taxes for the estimated sales of tobacco to actual tribal members. Further, the draft agreement requires the Tribe to verify its enrollment numbers and provide information requested by the state on the number of tribal members on an annual basis to calculate the estimated amount of sales to actual tribal members. This proposed agreement would require the tribal government to enact tribal legislation for the same amount of tobacco tax as the state government and serve as only a collection mechanism for the state department on revenue for all on-reservation tobacco sales with a ten-year period for the agreement.

Taxation issues between tribal governments and state governments continue to be an area of controversy, litigation, and negotiation. Attorneys working on both sides of the bargaining table must fully understand the contours of tribal sovereignty, tribal-state relations and the field of taxation under federal Indian law to effectively practice in this politically-charged legal area.

b. Tribal-State Revenue Sharing under Gaming Compacts

Another potential for controversy exists in the revenue sharing provisions of Tribal-State gaming compacts for Class III gaming under the Indian Gaming Regulatory Act (IGRA), 25 U.S.C. § 2701. With the *Seminole Tribe of Florida v. Florida,* 517 U.S. 44 (1996) decision by the U.S. Supreme Court, the provisions of the IGRA permitting a tribal government to file suit in federal court when a state failed to negotiate a Class III gaming compact in good faith were effectively stricken from the law. In the aftermath, some state governments have inserted revenue sharing provisions into tribal-state gaming compacts. The IGRA prohibits state officials from imposing "any tax, fee, charge or other assessment upon an Indian tribe or upon any other person or entity authorized by an Indian tribe to engage in a class III activity," 25 U.S.C. § 2710(d)(4). Further, state officials cannot condition negotiations for Class III gaming compacts upon assessing any of the above. IGRA does provide that a state official may negotiate costs for state regulation or enforcement of state civil and criminal laws under a Class III compact, 25 U.S.C. § 2710(d)(3)(C)(iii).

The Secretary of the Interior has final approval authority on all Tribal-State compacts and has taken the informal position that revenue sharing is allowed either to cover regulatory costs of the state under the gaming compact or where the tribal government is receiving a particular exclusivity benefit not available to other gaming operations from the state in the bargaining process. On the National Indian Gaming Commission (NIGC) web site, the Reading Room section includes a link to compacts between Tribal Nations and state governments. The compact approval letter from the Secretary of the Interior for the Pueblo of San Juan and New Mexico, dated October 1, 1997, indicated concerns surrounding the amount of revenue sharing and regulatory costs to the state, but the Secretary allowed the 45 day approval period to expire, providing a default approval of the compact. In California, revenue sharing provisions have become standard in gaming compacts with payments made directly to the state's general fund and to a special distribution fund that is divided up among the non-gaming tribal governments in the state. The ratified compacts are available on the California Gambling Control Commission web site.

Many of the federal land claims settlement acts for tribal governments on the east coast include specific provisions that impact tribal gaming opportunities. For example, the 1980 Maine Indian Claims Settlement Act provides that any general federal legislation for tribal governments will not apply to those in Maine unless specifically mentioned in the federal law, 25 U.S.C. § 1735(b). In *Passamaquoddy Tribe v. Maine*, 75 F.3d 784 (1st Cir. 1996), the federal court of appeals held that the 1988 Indian Gaming Regulatory Act did not apply to the tribal governments in Maine due to the above provision in the Maine Indian Lands Claims Settlement Act. In 1987, the Maine legislature did pass state laws authorizing issuance of licenses to the three tribal governments in the state to operate "high-stakes bingo," Me. Stat. Ann. Rev. 17 § 314-A. In recent years, attempts by Tribal Nations have failed to garner enough votes in Maine through state referendums to authorize an expansion of tribal gaming to Class III gaming.

One of the most successful gaming Tribes in the U.S. has been the Mashantucket Pequot Tribal Nation in Connecticut. The gaming compact entered into between the Tribe and the state has resulted in 25% to the state for every win at a slot machine along with other percentages based on free play games in the tribal gaming facility, Foxwoods Resort Casino. The amount received by the state in fiscal year 2010/2011 was reported to be $174 million according to the Connecticut Consumer Protection web page under tribal statistics for Foxwoods. This high percentage of revenue going straight to state coffers has motivated other state governments to seek a greater share of gaming revenues from tribal gaming enterprises across the country.

4. Tribal-State Co-Management Agreements

Opportunities exist for tribal-state cooperation on many issues common to both governments. For example, tribal colleges and state colleges may enter into articulation agreements to allow for students to transfer between degree programs from on-reservation education institutions to off-reservation state

Sisseton Wahpeton College Four Direction Drummers. Photo credit Stephen L. Jackson, Jr.

schools. The American Indian Higher Education Consortium (AIHEC) maintains a listing of tribal colleges with descriptions of articulation agreements entered into with area state educational institutions on its web page at: http://www.aihec.org/colleges/TCUprofiles.cfm. Promoting education is a common goal of both tribal and state governments that allows for the negotiation of articulation agreements.

Many other potential areas for collaboration exist. Tribal governments and state governments can enter into agreements regarding human services, child care services, environmental protection, and wildlife management, among other common interests. Federal agencies administer funding for many cooperative efforts between tribal and state governments. For example, the U.S. Department of Health and Human Services published in 2005, *Tribes and States*

Working Together: A Guide to Tribal-State Child Care Coordination. For eligibility to receive funding from the federal Child Care and Development Fund (CCDF), "[b]oth States and Tribes are required by Federal statute and CCDF regulations to describe within their CCDF two-year plans how they are coordinating with each other to provide child care services within their boundaries," according to page one of the Guide.

In sum, tribal governments and state governments are increasingly collaborating in areas of common interest and with the financial assistance of federal agencies. Jurisdictional and revenue issues continue to be hot topics with governmental sovereignty at stake. As permanent neighbors with citizens of both governments in their jurisdictions, tribal and state governments have a vested interest in cooperative relations.

Checkpoints

- The primary governmental relationship is between the tribal governments and the federal government. Due to the proximity between tribal governments and state governments, significant areas of collaboration around common concerns have developed in contemporary times.

- Tribal members have dual citizenship as citizens of the United States which incorporates state citizenship. Both tribal and state governments serve tribal members through governmental services.

- State governments have increasingly sought to tax activities within tribal territories. While there is no direct enforcement mechanism for such state taxation, the trend has been to enter into tribal-state tax agreements to satisfy the legal standards set forth by the U.S. Supreme Court.

Chapter 9

Sacred Sites and Cultural Property Protection

Roadmap

- Learn that tribal culture has a strong relationship with the stewardship of sacred sites and a geographically based sense of spirituality.

- Understand that due to the land loss by Tribal Nations, many sacred sites are now located on federal public lands and under the management authority of federal agencies.

- Understand that the U.S. Constitution has been interpreted by the U.S. Supreme Court to prioritize property ownership rights over spiritually based geographical tribal stewardship.

- Know that federal laws have been enacted to protect the human remains and funerary objects of tribal peoples and to provide support for tribal cultural protection offices.

This chapter will present the issues that tribal peoples face in the United States when seeking legal protection for sacred sites and cultural property. Law is necessarily the outgrowth of societal standards and concerns. U.S. law is based on an Anglo worldview and provides protection for religious freedom as understood from that worldview. The American Indian worldview on sacred sites is dissimilar in important respects from the worldview protected under U.S. property law and religious freedom. The use of cultural property under U.S. law as a commercial resource is also at odds with the American Indian view of cultural items and expression. Tribal laws may afford some protection to sacred sites and to cultural property, as will be discussed further in this chapter.

A. Lack of Protection of Sacred Sites and Limited Protection of Cultural Property under U.S. Law

The spirituality of American Indians has been explained as a geographical-based sense of stewardship and worship at sacred sites as contrasted with the European historical sense of religion that may be "practiced" at any location. This difference in perspective has led to a lack of legal protection in the U.S. for the continuation of Native spirituality at a sacred site where land ownership has changed hands. With the land loss from the allotment era in the late 1800s, many of the sacred sites stewarded by Tribal Nations for thousands of years became separated from tribal communities through transfer of ownership under U.S. property laws. Millions of acres of lands that were important to the tribal cycle of life and had been maintained for spiritual purposes suddenly had fences erected around them or subjected tribal peoples to trespassing charges for visiting those places.

Some of the medicine men and women across the country had continued to practice and pass on Native beliefs and ceremonies throughout the assimilation period and up to contemporary times. The journeys to sacred sites happened under cover of darkness when possible. Tribal people had secretly gathered and held ceremonial events even when such practices were outlawed by the U.S. government. With the civil rights movements in the late 1960s and the 1970s, tribal peoples began to seek rights of access and protection of sacred sites under U.S. laws to help restore traditional religious and spiritual practices at sacred sites located on lands outside of tribal ownership.

1. Efforts to Protect Sacred Sites

A tension exists in most tribal traditions between the confidentiality required to steward sacred sites and the disclosure of sacred site locations to assert cultural property protection under U.S. law. Often when the sacred site is in danger of desecration, tribal groups will come forward to reveal the sacredness of the endangered place and seek to protect the site for its spiritual purpose. In this section, three persistent efforts to protect sacred sites by tribal peoples will be discussed — the Chimney Rock area in Northern California, Bear's Lodge in the Black Hills of South Dakota and Wyoming (referred to as "Devils Tower" by the U.S. National Park Service), and the sacred mountain north of Flagstaff, Arizona (referred to by the U.S. Forest Service as the San Francisco Peaks composed of Humphrey Peak, Agassiz Peak, and Fremont Peak).

The sacred mountain is known and used by many of the area Tribal Nations and is called the Abalone Shell Mountain by the Navajo Nation; the Hopi Nation named it the Place of Snow on the Very Top; and it is called by the Havasupai Nation the Big Rock Mountain.

a. Litigation to Protect the Chimney Rock Area in Northern California

In 1982, the U.S. Forest Service in northern California adopted a plan to construct a paved road to allow timber harvesting in the Chimney Rock area of the Six Rivers National Forest where tribal ceremonies had been performed for centuries. The Yurok, Karok, Tolowa and other Indians had engaged in ceremonies at this sacred place and the Hoopa Valley Indian Reservation was adjacent to the national forest area. Litigation was initiated to halt the construction of the road in conjunction with the timber harvesting plan. Eventually, the issue was decided as a matter of federal law by the U.S. Supreme Court in *Lyng v. Northwest Indian Cemetery Protective Association*, 485 U.S. 439 (1988).

According to the U.S. Supreme Court opinion, a study in 1979 commissioned by the U.S. Forest Service found that the Chimney Rock area was "significant as an integral and indispensable part of Indian religious conceptualization and practice," 485 U.S. at 442. This study recommended that the road not be constructed because it would "cause serious and irreparable damage to the sacred areas which are an integral and necessary part of the belief systems and lifeway of the Northwest California Indian peoples," *Id.* Rejecting the recommendation, the U.S. Forest Service chose a construction route for the road with protective zones around the identified sacred sites along with approving a timber harvesting plan in the area. Tribal governments, tribal individuals, the National Congress of American Indians, conservation groups, civil rights organizations and the state of California filed suit in federal district court seeking a permanent injunction against the construction of the road and the timber harvesting plan.

After a permanent injunction was issued by the federal district court, the Ninth Circuit Court of Appeals affirmed the injunction in part and an appeal was taken to the U.S. Supreme Court. The U.S. Supreme Court based its ruling upon the question of whether the Free Exercise Clause of the First Amendment to the U.S. Constitution was violated by the proposed road and timber harvesting plan. Under previous decisions by the Court if there is a showing that government action places a burden on the exercise of religious practice in violation of the Free Exercise Clause, then the governmental action can go forward only if a compelling need is demonstrated, 485 U.S. at 447.

In the U.S. Supreme Court majority opinion authored by Justice Sandra Day O'Connor, the Court stated the following as central to its decision reversing the injunction.

> The Constitution does not permit government to discriminate against religions that treat particular physical sites as sacred, and a law prohibiting the Indian respondents from visiting the Chimney Rock area would raise a different set of constitutional questions. Whatever rights the Indians may have to the use of the area, however, those rights do not divest the Government of its right to use what is, after all, *its* land, 485 U.S. at 453 (emphasis in the original).

In the Court's opinion, the tribal peoples were not being deprived of their right to religious freedom, but instead were seeking to interfere with governmental action on governmental lands. Further, the U.S. Supreme Court opinion reviewed the 1978 American Indian Religious Freedom Act (AIRFA), 42 U.S.C. § 1996, and concluded that the AIRFA did not authorize any right to bring a case against the U.S. government. Rather, the AIRFA was simply a statement of policy and an obligation to consult with tribal leaders culminating in a 1979 report, 485 U.S. at 455.

In sum, the *Lyng* case stands for the U.S. Supreme Court holding that adverse governmental action to sacred sites on governmental lands does not violate the U.S. Constitution's Free Exercise Clause. This holding can be understood as the ordering of U.S. property rights above the spiritual rights of American Indians when sacred site locations are no longer on lands owned by tribal peoples. As a practical matter, the road at issue in the case was never constructed since part of the federal district court's injunction remained intact concerning non-compliance with federal laws prior to construction. As a legal precedent, the *Lyng* case leaves little hope for protection of a sacred site on federal lands for tribal peoples under the U.S. Constitution, based in part on the concern that giving tribal peoples a veto power over federal actions would create "special rights" not enjoyed by other religious groups

b. Litigation to Preserve Bear's Lodge in the Black Hills

For the Dakota, Lakota and Nakota peoples (commonly known as the "Sioux" Nation) and for many other Tribal Nations of the Plains, the Black Hills area is a sacred landscape and is a spiritual center for ceremonial activities, burials, social gatherings, medicine harvesting, and other spiritual activities. The natural earth features of the Black Hills correspond to constellations in the sky, contain a seasonal calendar for territorial movement on the Great Plains, and reflect the historical accounts of events that form the tribal worldview and spiritual philosophy for many of the Plains Tribal Nations. One of these natural features is "Bear's Lodge" which was formed in a sacred manner according to oral traditions. The Arapaho called it "Bear's Tipi"; the Crow referred to it as "Bear's House"; and the Kiowa named it "Tree Rock." In contemporary times, it is called Devil's Tower by the U.S. National Park Service and located within the U.S. Black Hills National Forest in Wyoming.

The U.S. claims title to the Black Hills National Forest in violation of the Fort Laramie Treaties of 1851 and 1868. In 1980, the U.S. Supreme Court held in *United States v. Sioux Nation of Indians*, 448 U.S. 371 (1980) that the U.S. government had wrongfully taken the Black Hills from the Sioux Nation and owed just compensation under the Fifth Amendment of the U.S. Constitution. The multimillion dollar amount has never been claimed by the tribal peoples in the lawsuit based upon spiritual principles and beliefs that Paha Sapa or the Black Hills are sacred lands that could not be purchased by the United States government.

As managed by the U.S. National Park Service (NPS), the sacred site known as Bear's Lodge became a popular destination for recreational rock climbers in the mid-1900s. Tribal peoples continued the historical ceremonial practices at Bear's Lodge in spite of the disruption by tourists and climbers at the site. When the NPS issued a mandatory ban on climbing the monument during the month of June in recognition of the ceremonial activities taking place at the sacred site, a group of recreational climbers successfully challenged the ban as violative of the Establishment Clause of the U.S. Constitution in *Bear Lodge Multiple Use Association v. Babbitt*, No. 96-CV-063-D (D. Wyo. Jun. 8, 1996) slip opinion. Under the Establishment Clause, the U.S. government is prohibited from giving preferential treatment to specific religious organizations. The Department of the Interior thereafter amended the NPS management plan and withdrew the mandatory climbing ban provision.

Subsequently, the NPS enforced the "Final Climbing Management Plan" (FCMP) as amended which provided that no new bolts or fixed pitons be hammered into the Devils Tower monument, required camouflage climbing equipment, seasonally closed climbing routes near raptor nests, and stated a voluntary ban on climbing for the month of June in recognition of tribal ceremonies at the sacred site. A non-profit organization representing recreational climbers and individual climbers brought suit a second time against the Secretary of the Interior in *Bear Lodge Multiple Use Association v. Babbitt*, 2 F.Supp.2d 1448 (1998). The second case challenged the FCMP as violative of the Establishment Clause with the voluntary June ban on climbing, challenged the NPS cultural interpretative program about tribal cultural and spiritual beliefs at the monument, and challenged the placement of NPS signs encouraging visitors to stay on the trails, 2 F.Supp.2d at 1451. The Cheyenne River Sioux Tribe, tribal spiritual leaders and individuals intervened in the lawsuit to add a first-hand account on the significance of Bear's Lodge. Additionally, national tribal organizations and religious freedom groups submitted briefs in support of the National Park Service's FCMP.

The federal district court reviewed the challenges to the interpretative program and the signs by the NPS and concluded that the climbers had not provided any evidence of actual harm. While the climbers argued that the cultural program served as a form of indoctrination to children visiting the monument, none of the climbers claimed to be parents of any such children and thus, they could not demonstrate the injury required to pursue a claim in court against the NPS. For this reason, the federal court held that the climbers lacked standing to bring a challenge to the cultural program, 2 F.Supp.2d at 1453. Similarly, the federal court found no injury to the climbers by the placement of the signs and no evidence was submitted that the signs actually stopped the climbers from leaving the trails.

As for the climbing ban in the month of June, the climbers asserted that the NPS be enjoined from ever imposing a mandatory ban and that both the voluntary and mandatory bans were violative of the Establishment Clause of the U.S. Constitution. The federal district court stated that the mandatory ban on commercial climbing was mooted since it had been withdrawn and suggested it would be unwise for it to be reinstated, 2 F.Supp.2d at 1452.

In analyzing the voluntary ban, the federal district court drew upon the test developed in the *Lemon v. Kurtzman*, 403 U.S. 602 (1971), case. The U.S. Supreme Court has set forth the principles to prevent governmental preference of religion or entanglement with religion under the *Lemon* test as follows: "a governmental action does not offend the Establishment Clause if it (1) has a secular purpose, (2) does not have the principal or primary effect of advancing or inhibiting religion, and (3) does not foster an excessive entanglement with religion," 2 F.Supp.2d at 1454. Applying this test to the voluntary climbing ban in the month of June at Devils Tower, the federal district court found that the NPS was accommodating tribal religious worship which served a legitimate secular purpose by removing barriers due to the public ownership of the sacred site, 2 F.Supp.2d at 1455. The court noted that the accommodation did not deprive the climbers of their legitimate use of the public lands and that there was no excessive entanglement by the NPS in monitoring the voluntary ban, 2 F.Supp.2d at 1456.

On appeal to the Tenth Circuit, the approval of the FCMP was upheld in *Bear Lodge Multiple Use Association v. Babbitt*, 175 F.3d 814 (10th Cir. 1999). The Tenth Circuit noted that the number of climbers on Devils Tower had increased substantially from 1973 with 312 climbers to an annual number of over 6,000 climbers, 175 F.3d at 818. In addition, the Court of Appeals highlighted that "[t]he named individual recreational climbers whose climbing activities have been undeterred by the FCMP have established no injury in fact and therefore do not have standing," 175 F.3d at 821. Likewise, no economic harm was asserted by the commercial guide who brought the case along with the climbers. Finding a lack of standing by the parties who brought the federal lawsuit, the Tenth Circuit affirmed the district court's opinion.

In conclusion, tribal peoples helped educate the National Park Service officials in the Black Hills National Forest who attempted to accommodate and recognize the use of a sacred site. This was challenged and under the U.S. Constitution, the NPS could only recommend that others voluntarily refrain from climbing on and disrupting the sacred site, Bear's Lodge, during ceremonial activities in the month of June.

c. Litigation over Recreational Activities and Artificial Snow on the San Francisco Peaks

The San Francisco Peaks, as they are now called by the U.S. Forest Service, are sacred mountains to many of the southwest Tribal Nations. In the desert terrain of the southwest, the Peaks are revered as home to spirit guardians who accept prayers and in turn form clouds with life-giving rain. Medicinal plants and special soils are gathered from the Peaks by tribal peoples in respectful ways to cure those below suffering from all manner of ailments. The Tribal Nations stewarding and utilizing the Peaks are numerous and include: the Navajo, Hopi, Havasupai, White Mountain Apache, Hualapai and Yavapai-Apache Nations. The San Francisco Peaks are composed of: Humphrey's Peak, Agassiz Peak, and Fremont Peak. Humphrey Peak is the highest of the three and is within the Coconino National Forest in northern Arizona.

Since the 1930s, the U.S. Forest Service has permitted downhill skiing and other recreational activities on Humphrey's Peak within 777 acres known as the Snowbowl. The southwest Tribal Nations have persistently asserted stewardship and challenged the actions of the U.S. Forest Service in expanding recreational activities at the Snowbowl, such as installing new lifts, slopes and facilities in the 1980s. In *Wilson v. Block,* 708 F2d 735, 739 (D.C. Cir. 1983), various Tribal Nations and tribal groups brought suit against the U.S. Forest Service and the U.S. Department of Agriculture when the agencies granted a permit to a private contractor operating the Snowbowl for expansion of the road to the facilities, construction of three additional lifts, clearing 50 acres of forest for new ski runs, and construction of a new day lodge. The lawsuit asserted violations of the American Indian Religious Freedom Act (AIRFA), of the fiduciary responsibilities of the U.S. government to American Indians, of the National Historic Preservation Act, of the National Environmental Policy Act (NEPA), and the Endangered Species Act, among other laws. The tribal plaintiffs' also asserted that their rights under the U.S. Constitution's First Amendment Free Exercise Clause and Establishment Clause were violated.

The Court of Appeals for the D.C. Circuit agreed with the lower court that the tribal plaintiffs' religious rights were not burdened by expansion of the Snowbowl facilities because "the government had not denied the Indians access to the Peaks or impaired their ability to gather sacred objects and conduct ceremonies, and thus had not burdened their beliefs or religious practices," 708 F.2d at 740. Furthermore, the D.C. Circuit Court found convincing that the tribal plaintiffs had continued their religious practices while the Snowbowl had been in operation for the previous fifty years and thus, the expansion could co-exist with the religious practices, 708 F.2d at 745. Taking each federal law argument in turn, the D.C. Circuit Court did not find any relief for the tribal plaintiffs to halt the expansion permit. In terms of the National Historic Preservation Act, the Chief Forester at the Peaks had complied with the district court's mandate to conduct a review and had concluded that the Peaks were ineligible for listing as a national historic site, 708 F.2d at 753–54. At the end of this lawsuit, the expansion was permitted against the strong opposition of the tribal peoples in the area.

Then in February 2005, the Forest Supervisor at the Peaks approved the proposal of the Snowbowl's private contractor to use recycled wastewater to make artificial snow to maintain the ski resort. After an administrative appeal to reverse the approval was denied, tribal groups, tribal governments, individuals and others again filed suit in federal court, *Navajo Nation v. U.S. Forest Service*, 408 F.Supp.2d 866 (D. Ariz. 2006). The case wound its way up from the federal district court which denied all of the plaintiffs' claims to the Ninth Circuit appeals court which partially granted relief under the Religious Freedom and Restoration Act of 1993 (RFRA), 42 U.S.C. § 2000bb et seq., *Navajo Nation v. U.S. Forest Service*, 479 F.3d 1024 (9th Cir. 2007), only to be heard again by a full panel of the Ninth Circuit to deny all of the tribal plaintiffs' claims. The initial lawsuit was filed in June of 2005 and the final decision by the en banc panel of the Ninth Circuit was issued on August 8, 2008—*Navajo Nation v. U.S. Forest Service*, 535 F.3d 1058 (9th Cir. 2008).

In the final decision by the full panel of the Ninth Circuit, the RFRA claim was analyzed to determine whether the tribal plaintiffs' had presented evidence that the use of the recycled wastewater to make artificial snow constituted a substantial burden on their free exercise of religion, 535 F.3d at 1068. The Ninth Circuit stated that if such evidence was presented, then the burden would shift to the federal government agency to demonstrate a compelling interest to go forward with the permit for the artificial snow, 535 F.3d at 1069. In determining whether a substantial burden would occur, the Ninth Circuit made the following findings.

> The only effect of the proposed upgrades is on the Plaintiffs' subjective, emotional religious experience. That is, the presence of recycled wastewater on the Peaks is offensive to the Plaintiffs' religious sensibilities. To plaintiffs, it will spiritually desecrate a sacred mountain and will decrease the spiritual fulfillment they get from practicing their religion on the mountain. Nevertheless, under Supreme Court precedent, the diminishment of spiritual fulfillment—serious though it may be—is not a "substantial burden" on the free exercise of religion, 535 F.3d at 1070.

Further, the Circuit Court held that the Religious Land Use and Institutionalized Persons Act of 2000 (RLUIPA) did not apply in the case when the government acted in a management capacity over its own land, 535 F.3d at 1077. In conclusion, the en banc panel of the Ninth Circuit affirmed the original decision by the federal district court denying relief to those bringing the lawsuit.

The tribal plaintiffs had brought the case finding offensive the proposal for spraying up to 1.5 million gallons of artificial snow on the sacred mountain made from raw sewage from the "waste discharged into Flagstaff's sewers by households, businesses, hospitals and industries" and then sent through a water treatment facility, 535 F.3d at 1083 (dissenting opinion). After the water treatment, the Arizona Department of Environmental Quality had issued a precaution that such treated sewage effluent not be ingested by humans, *Id.* (dissenting opinion). In the dissenting opinion, much of the testimony by the religious leaders of the southwestern Tribes was excerpted to demonstrate the depth of desecration that would be felt as a result of spraying sewage water on the holy mountain. The testimony discussed the sewage water from mortuaries, hospitals and restrooms as contaminating the mountain and the ceremonies that relied on the water and medicines from the Peaks:

> Foster, Nez, and Navajo practitioner Steven Begay testified that because they believe the mountain is an indivisible living entity, the entire mountain would be contaminated even if the millions of gallons of treated sewage effluent are put onto only one area of the Peaks. According to Foster, Nez, and Begay, there would be contamination even on those parts of the Peaks where the effluent would not come into physical contact with particular plants or ceremonial areas. To them, the contamination is not literal in the sense that a scientist would use the

term. Rather, the contamination represents the poisoning of a living being. In Foster's words, '[I]f someone were to get a prick or whatever from a contaminated needle, it doesn't matter what the percentage is, your whole body would then become contaminated. And that's what would happen to the mountain.' In Nez's words, 'All of it is holy. It is like a body. It is like our body. Every part of it is holy and sacred.' In Begay's words, 'All things that occur on the mountain are a part of the mountain, and so they will have connection to it. We don't separate the mountain,' 535 F.3d at 1104 (dissenting opinion).

After the final decision by the Ninth Circuit, the U.S. Supreme Court denied review of the decision and so, it stands to permit the proposal for artificial snowmaking from treated sewage effluent to be used at the Snowbowl for recreational skiers.

In reviewing these efforts by tribal peoples to protect sacred sites on lands that they no longer have legal ownership over, the observation can be made that legal protections for religious freedom in U.S. law do not provide sacred site protections for the religions of tribal peoples. The fundamental cultural difference in viewing sacred land areas as living, holy beings under tribal beliefs and U.S. property law based upon exploitation of land for commercial profit are fundamentally at odds when tribal peoples assert religious freedom claims based upon stewardship of sacred land areas. For further information on sacred site protection, the documentary, *In the Light of Reverence* (Bullfrog Films 2001), visually depicts tribal efforts to protect several sacred land areas in the United States.

One positive development occurred with the issuance of Presidential Executive Order No. 13007 directing all federal agencies to accommodate sacred sites. This has allowed for tribal consultation when a federal agency knows that a sacred site may be impacted by agency action. There is more work to be done as this area of law continues to develop.

B. Protection of Tribal Human Remains and Cultural Property

Along with the loss of stewardship to protect off-reservation sacred sites, a portion of the U.S. military, the scientific community, Indian hobbyists and artifact collectors for museums have engaged in looting tribal burial grounds. For example, the U.S. Surgeon General issued Circular No. 2 in 1867 to those interested in the "progress of medical science" to gather "typical crania of Indian tribes, specimens of their arms, dress, implements, rare articles of their diet, medicines, etc." and send them to the Army Medical Museum. One of the frequent complaints from tribal communities has been the extraction of Indian artifacts and remains from tribal gravesites on and off reservations dating back to the 1800s with no recourse for tribal families and governments. Tribal groups took a proactive role in lobbying for the passage of the 1990 federal Native American Graves Protection and Repatriation Act (NAGPRA), 25 U.S.C. § 3001 et seq. to stop this type of violation on federal and tribal lands.

Under the NAGPRA, federal agencies and museums receiving federal funding are required to document and publish notices of inventory regarding Native American human remains, funerary objects, sacred objects and other objects of cultural patrimony. The inventory should include the geographical and cultural affiliation of each item to the extent possible, 25 U.S.C. § 3003. Indian Tribes and Native Hawaiian organizations are to be notified of relevant inventories and may request additional information about listed items or remains, 25 U.S.C. § 3003(b)(2) and (d). The NAGPRA provides that expeditious repatriation of inventoried items or remains shall occur in consultation with the Tribal Nation, lineal descendant or Native Hawaiian organization that has established cultural affiliation, 25 U.S.C. § 3005(a). If the inventory does not establish cultural affiliation, then the claimant of the item or remains must "show cultural affiliation by a preponderance of the evidence based upon geographical, kinship, biological, archaeological, anthropological, linguistic, folkloric, oral traditional, historical, or other relevant information or expert opinion" to have the item or remains repatriated, 25 U.S.C. § 3005(a)(4).

Under the NAGPRA, a formal Review Committee was established with membership appointed by the Secretary of the Interior, 25 U.S.C. § 3006. According to the U.S. Department of the Interior's web site dedicated to National NAGPRA, the duties of the Review Committee involve facilitating the resolution of repatriation disputes and consideration of "requests for the disposition of culturally unidentifiable human remains." Additionally, the NAGPRA includes civil penalty provisions for any museum failing to comply with the inventory and repatriation directives, 25 U.S.C. § 3007(a). The Secretary of the Interior has discretion over issuing such penalties and factors under the NAGPRA for the amount to be assessed, 25 U.S.C. § 3007(b).

One notable exception to the reach of the NAGPRA's provisions is the Smithsonian Institution, which was specifically exempted from the legislation, 25 U.S.C. § 3001(4). Rather, a separate federal law was enacted when the National Museum of the American Indian was created as a subsidiary of the Smithsonian. Under 20 U.S.C. § 80q-9(a) and (c), the Secretary of the Smithsonian Institution was directed to inventory Indian human remains and funerary objects in its collections for return to the tribal descendants or tribal government with cultural affiliation established by a preponderance of the evidence standard.

In July 2010, the United States Government Accountability Office (GAO) released the report: *Native American Graves Protection and Repatriation Act— After Almost 20 Years Key Federal Agencies Still Have Not Fully Complied with the Act* (GAO-10-768). The GAO Report found that eight key federal agencies had not met their obligations under the NAGPRA and identified them as most compliant to least compliant on the introductory summary page of the Report. The most compliant, but not fully compliant agencies were: the U.S. Army Corps of Engineers, the U.S. Forest Service and the U.S. National Park Service doing the most work in identifying cultural items and human remains. Those which did some amount of work included the Bureau of Land Management, the Bureau of Reclamation and the Fish and Wildlife Service. The two federal agencies doing the least amount work to comply with the NAGPRA were the Bureau of Indian Affairs and the Tennessee Valley Authority.

Further, the GAO Report highlighted that a large number of tribal human remains and associated funerary objects inventoried had not been repatriated and none of the federal agencies were required to compile and report completed repatriations to anyone. "As a result, policymakers, Indian tribes, and Native Hawaiian organizations do not have access to readily available information about culturally affiliated NAGPRA items that have not been repatriated. According to officials, the remaining items have not been repatriated for a variety of reasons, such as a lack of repatriation requests and financial constraints," according to the July 2010 Report.

Another GAO Report dated May 2011 involving the return of tribal items and human remains was: *Smithsonian Institution—Much Work Still Needed to Identify and Repatriate Indian Human Remains and Objects* (GAO-11-515). In reviewing the slow process implemented by the Smithsonian for detailed case studies prior to repatriating funerary objects and human remains, the GAO concluded on the introductory summary page of the Report that "it could take several more decades to complete this process." Since the enactment of federal repatriation legislation for the Smithsonian, the Institution had "offered to repatriate over 5,000 human remains, which account for approximately one-third of the total estimated human remains in its collections." The number of funerary objects subject to repatriation was unknown since "the Smithsonian has no reliable estimate of the total number of such objects in its collections," the Report further stated. Much work has yet to be done in this area of repatriation and legal practitioners will continue to have a role to play in ensuring the return of tribal remains, artifacts and cultural property.

C. Tribal Cultural Protection Laws and Tribal Historic Preservation Offices

In response to the lack of cultural understanding and legal protection of tribal human remains, gravesites, sacred sites and cultural property, tribal governments have partnered with the National Park Service (NPS) to establish Tribal Historic Preservation Officers (THPO) through receipt of grant funds. Under the National Historic Preservation Act, 16 U.S.C. § 470a(d) and (e), the Secretary of the Interior was authorized in 1994 to begin assisting Tribal Nations in forming their own historic preservation programs, coordinating efforts between tribal, Native Hawaiian, state and federal preservation programs, and providing grants or loans to administer preservation programs. The Standing Rock Sioux Tribe's Tribal Historic Preservation web site provides that it was the first tribal preservation program established on August 14, 1996.

The National Association of Tribal Historic Preservation Officers (NATHPO) offers technical assistance and forums for THPOs to share best practices and consult on their collective and individual efforts. On the NATHPO web site, the three main principles guiding the national association are:

1. Tribal Sovereignty—the inherent right of Indian Nations to self-government.
2. Confidentiality—recognition of the need to respect the confidentiality of information regarding Native cultural and ceremonial practices and places of religious or cultural significance.
3. No boundaries—NATHPO recognizes that the cultural and heritage preservation interests of Indian Nations and their peoples often extend far beyond the boundaries of present-day reservations—often crossing state and national boundaries—and stands ready to assist in activities relating to transboundary cultural and environmental issues.

In addition to the development of formal Tribal Historic Preservation Officers, tribal governments have also been proactive in passing tribal laws on cultural property protection, sacred sites, tribal gravesites and the protection of cultural resources.

For example, the Hopland Band of Pomo Indians has enacted a Cultural Resources Management and Protection Code available publicly on the tribal web site. The Code defines cultural resources broadly as "any material remains of past human life or its associated activities which are of archaeological, historical, or cultural interest to the Tribe. Such material remains shall include, but are not limited to, abalone shells, pottery, basketry, bottles, weapons, weapon projectiles, tools, structures or portions of dwellings, burial sites, cemeteries, human skeletal remains, associated or unassociated funerary objects, clothing, artwork, ceremonial objects, sacred objects, or any part of these items," Title 20 Chapter 1 Section 3.1 (2006).

Tribal laws and THPOs are serving to protect tribal cultural resources and in the process, provide cultural education to the agencies of the U.S. government and to U.S. citizens on the tribal worldview on sacred sites, tribal stewardship views, and intercultural dialogue on cultural significance. This is an evolving area of law that will continue to develop and will require competent legal practitioners to serve on the forefront of articulating legal protections applicable to tribal communities.

Checkpoints

- American Indian spiritual principles connected to sacred sites are not commonly understood or protected in U.S. law. Cross-cultural understanding is necessary to provide greater legal protections.

- Tribal Nations continue to assert legal arguments and seek federal policy changes to protect spiritually, culturally and historically important geographical sites.

- With the enactment of the Native American Graves Protection and Repatriation Act (NAGPRA), the looting of tribal cemeteries and the unauthorized collection of ancestral remains are federal offenses on tribal and federal lands. Federally-funded museums have obligations under the law to inventory tribal items and respond to requests for repatriation of tribal cultural patrimonial items.

- Tribal Historic Preservation Officers are operating to ensure that tribal cultural property is recognized and preserved. Tribes are developing cultural resource protection laws.

Chapter 10

International Indigenous Issues and Tribal Nations

Roadmap

- Learn about the international underpinnings of the relationship between Tribal Nations and the United States.

- Learn about the early efforts to join international organizations by tribal leaders and share the Indigenous viewpoint on global affairs.

- Understand the development in the U.S. of the American Indian Movement and the connection to international Indigenous collaborations.

- Know the major international documents that support Indigenous human rights.

In this chapter, the history of the interaction between indigenous peoples, particularly from North America, and the world organizations of nation-states will be discussed. The tribal peoples in the United States have often taken a leadership role in advancing global indigenous rights. As greater means of communication become available, indigenous peoples around the world are sharing common issues of land stewardship, survival from assimilation policies, protection of cultural resources, assertion of human rights, and adaptation to changing economics.

A. Early Efforts to Join World Organizations

As Tribal Nations in the United States experienced severe oppression and economic devastation in the late 1800s and early 1900s, many tribal leaders continued to assert tribal sovereignty and advocate from the legal agreements entered into with the U.S. Around the globe, indigenous leaders shared this same experience in asserting their rights in dealing with Great Britain and its governmental offspring. For example, the Maori of New Zealand entered into the Treaty of Waitangi in 1840 with officials from Great Britain. Where legal agreements were not entered into, warfare ensued as indigenous peoples sought to protect their homes, families, lands, and ways of life from European invasion in Africa, Australia, the Philippines, North America, and South America.

Two documented accounts of indigenous leaders seeking to be heard at the League of Nations in the early 1920s attest to the tenacity of asserting nation-state status by indigenous peoples. A leader and advocate for the Haudenosaunee, also known as the Iroquois Confederacy of the Six Nations, Deskaheh Levi General traveled to Geneva, Switzerland in 1923 and spent a year seeking an audience and relief on behalf of his people in response to the actions of Canada and the British monarchy. He was blocked from presenting his case to the League of Nations by those nation-states. Another attempt to gain access to the League of Nations was made by the Maori leader T.W. Ratana in 1925. He also was denied access to protest the breaking of the Treaty of Waitangi. These early efforts demonstrate the firm belief that indigenous peoples refused to surrender to outside forces and maintained their sense of entitlement to participate on the global level.

B. Contemporary Indigenous Rights Movements

With the civil rights movements occurring in the United States in the late 1960s and the 1970s, groups who had experienced political and economic exclusion were engaging in civil disobedience and leading protest marches. American Indians raised in urban areas as a result of the 1950s BIA Relocation Program became aware of these strategies to voice feelings of being oppressed and disempowered. One of the most well-known political groups emerging from this sense of urban unrest was known as the American Indian Movement (AIM). Engaging in violent confrontations as well as organizing long distance peaceful walks, AIM brought media and public attention to the issues facing American Indians on reservations and throughout the country.

1. The American Indian Movement's Impact on Collective Rights

AIM provided a way for urban and reservation Indians to stand together to voice disagreement over U.S. Indian policy and the lack of economic opportunity for Indian people. In 1973, the AIM gathered together at the village of Wounded Knee on the Pine Ridge Reservation to serve as protection against the local tribal law enforcement. The U.S. government sent in officers of the Federal Bureau of Investigation (FBI) and U.S. Marshals to surround those gathered together. After over seventy days, the AIM occupation of Wounded Knee ended, but the group had held off over 300 armed federal troops, state troops and antagonistic tribal officers. Wounded Knee was the historic site of the massacre on December 29, 1890 of unarmed men, women and children trying to reach the safety of the Pine Ridge Reservation only to be gunned down by U.S. cavalry. The 1973 occupation of Wounded Knee was a reminder that the U.S. government had failed to fulfill its promises in treaties, had failed to provide the necessary assistance to American Indian peoples, and had continued to view American Indians as the enemy, rather than the ally.

2. Formation of the International Indian Treaty Council and NGO Status

Following the occupation, the Standing Rock Sioux Tribal Council called together a conference on enforcement of the treaties entered into between Tribal Nations and the United States. Leading international law scholars were invited and met with tribal peoples from across the country at the conference. From this event, the International Indian Treaty Council (IITC) was formed and a declaration adopted, "Declaration of Continuing Independence by the First International Indian Treaty Council at Standing Rock Indian Country June 1974." The first order of business for the IITC was to attain Non-Government Organization (NGO) status with the United Nations to begin presenting the issues faced by Tribal Nations and peoples to the international community.

The IITC successfully attained NGO status to the United Nations Economic and Social Council (ECOSOC) in 1977. To garner attention on indigenous people's issues, the IITC organized a conference in Geneva, Switzerland titled, "International NGO Conference On Discrimination Against Indigenous Populations In the Americas— 1977." The focus was on the poor economic, political, legal, and social conditions for the indigenous peoples of the Western Hemisphere due to European invasion and subsequent establishment of settler governments. Over 100 indigenous delegates attended to provide testimony before the UN officials present. A co-sponsor of the conference was the ECOSOC Sub-Committee on Racism, Racial Discrimination, Apartheid, and Decolonization of the Special Committee on Human Rights. The four-day conference from Sept. 20–23, 1977 culminated in a Report that included a Final Resolution and a Declaration by those in attendance. In the Final Resolution on page 22 of the Report, the attendance at the conference was reported as follows.

For the first time, the widest and most united representation of indigenous nations and peoples, from the Northern to the most Southern tip and from the far West to the East of the Americas took part in the Conference. They included representatives of more than 60 Nations and peoples, from fifteen countries (Argentina, Bolivia, Canada, Chile, Costa Rica, Guatemala, Ecuador, Mexico, Nicaragua, Panama, Paraguay, Peru, Surinam, United States of America, Venezuela).

It is regretted that some delegates were prevented by their governments from attending.

At the center of this historic meeting was a declaration on the human rights, environmental rights, legal, political, and social rights being asserted by indigenous populations.

The work of the Geneva conference continued pursuant to the ECOSOC Resolution 1982/34 establishing the Working Group on Indigenous Populations under the Sub-Commission on the Promotion and Protection of Human Rights. On the website of the Working Group, its two primary mandates were: "to review developments pertaining to the promotion and protection of human rights and fundamental freedoms of indigenous peoples" and "to give attention to the evolution of international standards concerning indigenous rights."

C. Significant International Indigenous Human Rights Instruments and Developments

The international landscape for indigenous human rights has changed considerably in the last several decades due to the increased vocalization from indigenous peoples on the conditions they face. From the Western Hemisphere, efforts have been made by indigenous peoples to rejoin the international community of nations on an equal basis. This goal has not been attained to date. For Tribal Nations in mid-North America, the options are: to work through organizations with NGO status within the UN; to work in collaboration with the United States of America to present issues on an international scale; or to seek partnerships with others recognized within the United Nations nation-state structure to raise issues.

As the UN Working Group on Indigenous Populations continued to document and research the status of indigenous peoples around the world, four major developments occurred within the UN structure to support inclusion of these peoples. One was the revisions and work on a declaration embodying the human rights to be accorded indigenous peoples, the second was the establishment of the UN Permanent Forum on Indigenous Issues, the third was the appointment of a Special Rapporteur on the rights of indigenous peoples by the Commission on Human Rights, and fourth was the creation of the Expert Mechanism on the Rights of Indigenous Peoples. As indigenous organizations and Tribal Nations worked within the UN system, the ability to respond to U.S. Indian policy via reporting requirements in international conventions has become a further means of asserting international human rights standards for American Indians.

1. UN Special Rapporteur on the Rights of Indigenous Peoples

In 2001, the Commission on Human Rights appointed a Special Rapporteur on the Rights of Indigenous Peoples (Special Rapporteur) to travel, conduct investigations, and report on the situations of indigenous peoples. In the mandate issued by the Human Rights Council in Resolution 6/12 of September 28, 2007, the Special Rapporteur was directed to collaborate with the UN Permanent Forum on Indigenous Issues and the Expert Mechanism on the Rights of Indigenous Peoples to protect human rights and provide best practices to nation-states. The Special Rapporteur is empowered to investigate alleged violations of the human rights of indigenous peoples and to request from the involved governments documents and communications as necessary. In this manner, the Special Rapporteur acts as a frontline representative of the Human Rights Council to be dispatched when a human rights crisis may arise involving indigenous peoples around the globe.

2. UN Permanent Forum on Indigenous Issues

In 2002, the United Nations Permanent Forum on Indigenous Issues (Permanent Forum) held its first meeting as an advisory body within the UN Economic and Social Council to provide opportunities for indigenous leadership to provide input to the United Nations. The mandate of the Permanent Forum is three-fold according to its website—to "provide expert advice and recommendations on indigenous issues to the Council, as well as to programmes, funds and agencies of the United Nations, through the Council"; to "raise awareness and promote the integration and coordination of activities related to indigenous issues within the UN system"; and to "prepare and disseminate information on indigenous issues."

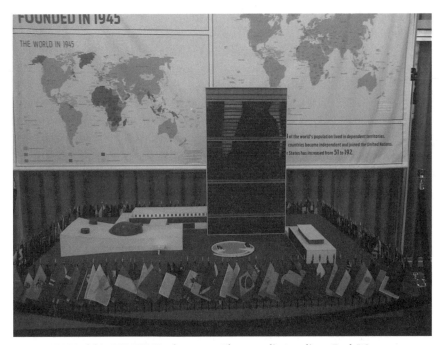

UN Model in NY UN Headquarters. Photo credit Angelique EagleWoman.

3. UN Declaration on the Rights of Indigenous Peoples

As indigenous peoples around the globe continued to give voice to their issues and the demand for basic human rights, the principles in the declaration considered at the 1977 Geneva conference became a focal point for unified action. On September 13, 2007, thirty years after that conference, the UN General Assembly adopted the UN Declaration on the Rights of Indigenous Peoples (UN DRIP), G.A. Res. 61/295, UNDOC A/RES/61/295. The original vote was 143 countries in support, 4 countries in opposition and 11 countries abstaining (including the Russian Federation). The four countries opposed during the adoption vote were Australia, Canada, New Zealand and the United States of America. All four subsequently have endorsed the UN DRIP in recent years.

The UN DRIP is a historic document and unique human rights instrument as the first to recognize collective human rights in addition to individual human rights. The Declaration serves as a floor for human rights of indigenous peoples around the world. Key features of the UN DRIP include: Article 3 recognizing the right to self-determination in pursuing political, economic, social and cultural direction; Article 8 containing the right "not to be subjected to forced assimilation or destruction of their culture"; Article 19 stating that nation-states shall adhere to the process of obtaining the "free, prior and informed consent" of indigenous peoples before taking action impacting them; Article 26 acknowledging that "indigenous peoples have the right to the lands, territories and resources which they have traditionally owned, occupied, or otherwise used or acquired"; and Article 37 calling for enforcement of "treaties, agreements and other constructive arrangements" entered into between indigenous peoples and nation-states.

The UN Declaration on the Rights of Indigenous Peoples is a set of guiding principles adopted by a strong consensus of the nation-states around the globe. These minimum standards of human rights for indigenous peoples will continue to transform the relations between indigenous peoples and nation-states in the years to come. The impact of the UN DRIP has yet to be realized for the Tribal Nations in relationship with the United States. Legal scholars have encouraged Tribal Nations to consider asserting indigenous collective rights identified in the UN DRIP when defending active claims against the United States to begin bringing those international indigenous rights to life.

4. UN Expert Mechanism on the Rights of Indigenous Peoples

The UN Human Rights Council pursuant to Resolution 6/36 on December 14, 2007 formed the Expert Mechanism on the Rights of Indigenous Peoples (Expert Mechanism). The purpose of the Expert Mechanism is to provide research, studies and recommendations to the Council. The first study of the Expert Mechanism was concluded in 2009 on the right to education for indigenous peoples with recommendations to further increase educational attainment. The second study was released in September of 2011 regarding indigenous peoples' right to participate in decision-making.

Five members compose the Expert Mechanism through appointment by the Human Rights Council. Both the Special Rapporteur and a member of the Permanent Forum are invited to attend the Expert Mechanism's annual July meeting where representatives of indigenous organizations, nation-state representatives, indigenous individuals, and other interested persons and organizations may take part. Through these four developments within the UN structure, Tribal Nations and indigenous peoples have greater opportunities to be heard on an international level.

5. The United States and UN Conventions Impacting Indian Policy

For Tribal Nations in relations with the United States, the UN Conventions that the United States has agreed to uphold may provide ways to influence U.S. Indian policy. For example, the United States has ratified and joined the UN Convention on the Elimination of Racial Discrimination (UN CERD) on September 28, 1966. The Convention is monitored by the Committee on the Elimination of Racial Discrimination which periodically requires nation-states bound by the Convention to submit progress reports. Additionally, organizations and individuals may file complaints or companion reports to the Committee on the actions of nation-states during the periodic review. The IITC and others have filed companion reports in coordination with the U.S. reporting requirement.

For example on March 10, 2006, the Committee on the Elimination of Racial Discrimination sent out a strongly worded decision to the United States concerning the unlawful seizure of the aboriginal lands of the Western Shoshone Nation and directed the U.S. to halt further desecration of those lands from military weapon testing, to immediately begin a dialogue with the Western Shoshone Peoples for a resolution to the land claim dispute in accordance with due process requirements, and to stop further imposition of fees on the use of the aboriginal lands by the Western Shoshone Peoples.

The Committee has also sent letters of concern over U.S. governmental actions regarding the Ski Resort at the San Francisco Peaks, discussed in Chapter 9. In a letter dated March 1, 2013, the Committee issued an "early warning and urgent action" communication to the United States government regarding: "the situation of the Kikapoo Traditional Tribe of Texas, the Ysleta del Sur Pueblo (Tigua) and the Lipan Apache (Ndé) indigenous communities in relation to the construction of the Texas-Mexico border wall," CERD 82nd/GH/CR/MN. These letters regarding the U.S. government's actions towards Tribal Nations are available on the Committee on the Elimination of Racial Discrimination—Early Warning Measures and Urgent Procedures web site at: http://www2.ohchr.org/english/bodies/cerd/early-warning.htm.

These letters demonstrate the international implications of U.S. Indian policy and allow for human rights protections to be accorded through the UN Conventions entered into by the U.S. As Tribal Nations continue to work within international forums, the UN Conventions binding upon the U.S. may be utilized to undo the negative aspects of past U.S. Indian policy and law.

D. Development of Other International Instruments on the Rights of Indigenous Peoples

While the United Nations continues to be the supreme international body establishing legal principles for member nation-states, there exist many other international and regional organizations that provide standards and conventions for member countries. This section will discuss a few significant developments for indigenous peoples through the International Labour Organisation, the Organization of American States, and the United League of Indigenous Nations.

1. The Conventions of the International Labour Organisation

The International Labour Organisation (ILO) in 1957 adopted C107 Indigenous and Tribal Populations Convention with the goal of integrating these identified populations into the mainstream of national societies. Article 2 contained the provisions directing nation-states to provide for national integration of indigenous populations and Article 3 included the further guideline that measures adopted should not prolong a state of separation for these populations. Evolution on the understanding of collective human rights for indigenous and tribal peoples led the ILO to adopt a new convention in 1989.

In 1989, the ILO adopted C169 Indigenous and Tribal Peoples Convention with less emphasis on national integration. Article 7 of the 1989 Convention is congruent with respect for indigenous and tribal peoples ability to chart their own economic, social and political directions. It provides in subsection (1):

> The peoples concerned shall have the right to decide their own priorities for the process of development as it affects their lives, beliefs, institutions and spiritual well-being and the lands they occupy or otherwise use, and to exercise control, to the extent possible, over their own economic, social and cultural development. In addition, they shall participate in the formulation, implementation and evaluation of plans and programmes for national and regional development which may affect them directly.

As international statements of indigenous and tribal peoples' rights, the ILO Conventions demonstrate the significant change in perspectives as understandings have developed on the collective nature and persistence of indigenous peoples worldwide.

2. Organization of American States' Draft American Declaration on the Rights of Indigenous Peoples

The nation-states in the Western Hemisphere compose the regional Organization of American States (OAS), including the United States of America. In 1948 with the signing of the OAS charter, the member nation-states adopted the American Declaration on the Rights and Duties of Man focused on individual rights, including the United States. In addition, the Inter-American Commission on Human Rights (IACHR) was established in 1959 and its purpose has expanded to provide for consideration of individual petitions, monitoring of human rights situations in nation-states in the Americas, and supporting the thematic priorities of the OAS. The United States has not ratified the 1969 American Convention on Human Rights which empowers the Inter-American Court of Human Rights to resolve violations under that Convention.

With the international movement towards collective human rights and the issues arising in member nation-states regarding indigenous peoples in the Western Hemisphere, the OAS has established a Working Group on the Draft American Declaration on the Rights of Indigenous Peoples. Without the adoption of this Declaration, the Inter-American Commission on Human Rights (IACHR) has applied other standards binding the nation-states involved in alleged human rights violations. For example, the IACHR issued a final decision, Report No. 75/02, December 27, 2002, in the case brought by Mary and Carrie Dann of the Western Shoshone as indigenous people against the United States for human rights violations under the American Declaration on the Rights and Duties of Man that the U.S. was bound by. Other Tribal Nations may seek to have their claims heard in the IACHR.

3. United League of Indigenous Nations Treaty and Organization

On August 1, 2007, a treaty was entered into to form the United League of Indigenous Nations (ULIN) between indigenous nations. The eleven signatory indigenous nations came from the United States, Canada, Australia, and New Zealand. The purpose of the treaty was to formally develop mutual covenants to promote each nation's self-determination and sovereignty. On the ULIN website is the full text of the treaty. The signatory nations pledged: "[t]o establish supportive bonds among signatory indigenous Nations in order to secure, recover, and promote, through political, social, cultural and economic unity, the rights of all our peoples, the protection and recovery of our homelands and for the well-being of all our future generations."

The concept of the ULIN treaty was developed from the National Congress of the American Indians (NCAI)'s Special Committee on Indigenous Nation Relationships. The ULIN has held its meetings during the NCAI's Annual and Mid Year Conferences. Within the ULIN, the League has working groups established on the issues of cultural property protection, trade, climate change, border crossing, and indigenous nations relations. The ULIN represents a movement toward both re-establishing the international bonds between indigenous and Tribal Nations that pre-existed European invasions and creating new bonds based on common issues faced across nation-state borders by indigenous peoples.

As this Chapter demonstrates, the international connections and activity of Tribal Nations as indigenous peoples of North America continues to build and strengthen bonds around the globe. In addition, the international human rights principles developing to embrace collective rights will likely have potential positive impacts for the relationships between Tribal Nations and the United States.

Checkpoints

- American Indian leaders have persistently asserted tribal sovereignty and treaty rights in the U.S. and in international forums. Tribal Nations have not assented to a status as less than full sovereigns.

- Tribal leaders have been engaged with the United Nations and worked with other indigenous peoples around the world to establish permanent means of communication within the organization.

- One of the most important international documents on indigenous human rights is the UN Declaration on the Rights of Indigenous Peoples (UN DRIP) approved on September 13, 2007. The UN DRIP will continue to have significant influence on the relationships between Tribal Nations and the United States.

- Alliances and confederacies are traditional governance activities of Tribal Nations and entering into treaties, conventions, and agreements based on mutual peaceful relations is a practice that will continue into the foreseeable future.

Mastering American Indian Law Master Checklist

After working through this book, you should be able to understand the following concepts set forth in the preceding chapters.

Chapter 1 • Introduction to American Indian Law

☐ Tribal governments create tribal law through legislation, judicial opinions, agency decisions, regulations, and adhering to traditional cultural norms and principle.

☐ Federal Indian law is developed through all three branches of the U.S. government. U.S. Indian policy eras frame major legislation and interactions between the U.S. and Tribal Nations.

☐ The Marshall Trilogy of cases is considered the foundation of federal Indian law.

☐ American Indian is a legal definition pursuant to tribal citizenship/enrollment laws and, in some instances, federal law.

Chapter 2 • American Indian Property Law

☐ Historical tribal property systems of ownership and territorial stewardship form the basis of contemporary tribal property law.

☐ Federal law has limited tribal autonomy over tribal property law, including limitations on the sale or alienation of tribal land.

☐ As a result of allotment, most tribal land bases have been divided into small parcels and are held in trust status under the management of the U.S. government.

☐ Extensive federal laws and regulations are involved in the leasing or use of tribal lands in trust or restricted status.

Chapter 3 • Criminal Jurisdiction in Indian Country

☐ For crimes occurring in Indian Country, an analysis of the race of the perpetrator and victim is necessary to determine the proper prosecuting authority.

☐ Early federal Indian law established federal criminal jurisdiction in Indian Country over felony level crimes committed by American Indians.

☐ The U.S. Supreme Court has held that tribal governments lost the authority to prosecute non-Indians committing crimes in Indian Country.

☐ Federal law recognizes inherent tribal authority over all Indians committing crimes in Indian Country and in special circumstances over non-Indians committing domestic violence against American Indians in Indian Country.

☐ As part of the U.S. Indian policy of termination, the federal Public Law 280 was enacted delegating federal criminal authority to certain state governments in Indian Country.

☐ Tribal governments share concurrent criminal jurisdiction with federal and/or state governments for crimes committed by American Indians in Indian Country.

☐ The criminal sentencing authority of Tribal Courts is limited by federal law.

Chapter 4 • Tribal Government, Civil Jurisdiction and Regulation

☐ Tribal governance has responded to shifting U.S. Indian policy eras.

☐ Many tribal governments have adopted tribal constitutions modeled upon the U.S. Constitution, but are not constrained by the U.S. Constitution in the exercise of tribal power.

☐ The U.S. Supreme Court has held that tribal authority is limited for civil regulatory actions involving non-Indians conducting activities on fee lands within Indian country.

☐ Tribal governments work closely with the U.S. Bureau of Indian Affairs to provide basic social and other services to tribal members.

Chapter 5 • Tribal Business, Industries and Best Commercial Practices

☐ The norm for tribal business is the tribal government-owned corporation, although variations exist under tribal, state and federal law.

☐ Alaska Native Corporations are operated under state law and authorized through federal legislation as part of the Alaska Native Claims Settlement Act.

☐ Federal incentives provide opportunities for tribal businesses to engage in economic development in usually economically-depressed communities.

☐ Tribal entities are covered by tribal sovereign immunity unless such immunity is expressly waived in a document or by federal or tribal law.

☐ The tribal gaming industry is federally regulated under the Indian Gaming Regulatory Act and tribal regulatory agencies.

Chapter 6 • Family Law in Tribal Communities

☐ Historically, tribal familial disputes were resolved using restorative justice principles.

☐ The U.S. Indian policy era of assimilation caused severe and long-lasting disruption to domestic tribal lifeways.

☐ The Indian Child Welfare Act was enacted to prevent the removal of American Indian children from tribal relations and to rehabilitate tribal families to keep the family intact.

☐ Tribal Courts are competent courts and bear the primary responsibility of handling family issues in tribal communities.

Chapter 7 • Natural Resources in Indian Country

☐ Tribal natural resources on trust lands are subject to extensive federal laws and regulations administered by the Department of the Interior.

☐ Tribal governments continue to seek greater management authority over natural resource and energy development from tribal lands.

☐ Tribal Nations collaborate with the U.S. Environmental Protection Agency to implement federal programs and tribal laws protecting tribal water, air, and lands.

☐ Tribal natural resources departments provide stewardship over tribal lands and treaty fishing, hunting, and gathering activities.

Chapter 8 • Tribal-State Relations

☐ Tribal-U.S. relations are the primary level of governmental interaction. Tribal-state relations have developed through the necessity of sharing citizens and common interests.

☐ Taxation has been an on-going area of negotiation between tribal and state governments.

☐ Formalized agreements between tribal governments and state governments provide regulatory certainty and mutual benefits.

Chapter 9 • Sacred Sites and Cultural Property Protection

☐ Central to tribal spirituality is the responsibility to steward sacred sites and honor the connection between the earth and humans.

☐ U.S. courts have interpreted the U.S. Constitution's religious guarantees as inapplicable to legal challenges brought by Tribes to preserve sacred sites located on federal public lands.

☐ Federal laws have been enacted providing protection against the looting of tribal cemeteries and providing for the return of tribal human remains and cultural items.

☐ Tribal laws have been developed to protection cultural resources and to implement Tribal Historic Preservation Offices.

Chapter 10 • International Indigenous Issues and Tribal Nations

- ☐ International law underlies the treaty-making between Tribal Nations and the U.S.
- ☐ Since the 1970s, Tribal leaders have been increasingly engaged at the United Nations with other indigenous leaders from around the world.
- ☐ A fundamental shift occurred with the adoption of the UN Declaration on the Rights of Indigenous Peoples in establishing a minimum for indigenous human rights worldwide.
- ☐ Tribal Nations continue to seek international alliances and confederacies based upon the kinship worldview.

Index